GUARANTEED INCOME FOR LIFE

How Variable Annuities
Can Cut Your Taxes,
Pay You Every Year
of Your Life,
and Bring You
Financial Peace of Mind

MICHAEL F. LANE

McGraw-Hill
New York San Francisco Washington, DC Auckland Bogotá
Caracas Lisbon London Madrid Mexico City Milan
Montreal New Delhi San Juan Singapore
Sydney Tokyo Toronto

Library of Congress Cataloging-in-Publication Data

Lane, Michael.
    Guaranteed income for life / by Michael Lane.
        p. cm.
    ISBN 0-07-038297-2
    1. Variable annuities.   I. Title.
    HG8790.L345   1998
    368.3 ' 75—dc21   98–3163
                                                                        CIP

McGraw-Hill

A Division of The **McGraw·Hill** Companies

1 2 3 4 5 6 7 8 9 0   DOC/DOC   9 0 3 2 1 0 9 8

ISBN 0-07-038297-2

*The sponsoring editor for this book was Stephen Isaacs, the editing supervisor was
Patricia V. Amoroso, and the production supervisor was Suzanne W. B. Rapcavage.
It was set in Palatino by Carol Barnstable of Carol Graphics.*

Printed and bound by R.R. Donnelley & Sons Company.

This publication is designed to provide accurate and authoritative
information in regard to the subject matter covered. It is sold with the
understanding that the publisher is not engaged in rendering legal,
accounting, or other professional service. If legal advice or other expert
assistance is required, the services of a competent professional person should
be sought.
            —*From a declaration of principles jointly adopted by a committee
            of the American Bar Association and a committee of publishers.*

 This book is printed on recycled, acid-free paper containing a
minimum of 50% recycled de-inked fiber.

McGraw-Hill books are available at special quantity discounts to use as
premiums and sales promotions, or for use in corporate training programs.
For more information, please write to the Director of Special Sales, McGraw-
Hill, 11 West 19th Street, New York, NY 10011. Or contact your local
bookstore.

CONTENTS

APPENDIXES

INTRODUCTION

Variable Annuity Investing: an investment strategy that increases net investment returns. The payoff: greater probability of economic freedom at retirement.

What is a variable annuity? Should I buy one? How do I know I have the right one? What effects do the new tax law changes have on my existing variable annuities? Are mutual funds better? How can I supplement my existing retirement plan? Am I paying too much and what can I do to lower my costs? What is a sub-account? What is the best settlement option? How can I analyze annuity companies? What are the best variable annuities? How do I find an advisor who understands variable annuities? Where can I go for help?

If you need answers to these questions, then you have purchased the right book.

Hello, my name is Michael Lane. I am President of AEGON Financial Services Group, Inc., Advisor Resources, located in Louisville, Kentucky. My firm is focused on helping people like you and professional investment advisors build successful investment solutions. Both individual investors and investment advisors who have followed the steps we are about to show you tell us this approach has made a significant difference in their financial well-being. We are confident the approach detailed in this book can do the same for you.

You will learn how to invest successfully using one of the most exciting investment products since the mutual fund. We will back up our claims with evidence every step of the way. The book is designed to encourage you and give you confidence as you make progress along your own investment path to a secure future.

I've written this book for several different types of readers. If you already own a variable annuity and have achieved success as an investor, this book can help you be even more successful. If you are contemplating the purchase of a variable annuity and want current information, this book will give you the facts and help you with your decision. If you are an investment advisor and are seeking a reliable guide to success for your clients, this is the road map you've been looking for.

PATH TO A SECURE FUTURE

Why learn more about annuities? Let's say you are a 35-year-old investing $10,000 in a low-cost tax-deferred variable annuity, and you're fortunate to get a return of 12 percent. By your 65th birthday, you could accumulate over $240,000. If you are able to add $5,000 a year all along the way, your $160,000 of total invested capital, compounding tax-free, could balloon to over $1,282,558. If you continue working and don't retire until age 70, your variable annuity could hold over $2,224,249. That's what's possible by investing in a variable annuity. Interested in learning more?

The focus of this book is primarily on *variable annuities,* investment methods used inside the variable annuity, and the role annuities play today in tax-efficient investment strategies.

The 23 chapters in this book present a logical approach to creating a successful variable annuity portfolio. Each chapter is also designed to stand alone. Use the book again and again as a resource handbook.

Before we get started, I would like to address the biggest concern that you as an investor will probably face in the years to come: how to build an investment portfolio that you can't outlive—ever!

Of concern to most investors is the very real possibility of outliving their retirement funds. Inflation doesn't stop, of course, the day of retirement. And for many people, the time spent in retirement will be nearly as long as the time spent in the work force. Without careful planning, retirees will face the prospect of running out of money before they run out of time. Most investment plans will run out of money at or before your life expectancy age, and what if you live 10 or 20 years longer? You'll have significant money problems. A technique called annuitization can help address this issue by guaranteeing payments that will continue *for the rest of your life, no matter how long that is.*

Investing in annuities resolves the biggest fear most people have— outliving their retirement dollars. What if that concern could be entirely eradicated? What if it could be guaranteed that, should you live to be 110, you will continue to receive uninterrupted income? That's within your grasp with a variable annuity.

My goals are to educate you on the appropriate uses of annuities so you'll have the information necessary to make successful decisions, and to provide your financial advisors with accurate, up-to-date information so they can assist you in making the very best decisions possible.

By the time you finish reading this book, you will know far more than 99 percent of stockbrokers on Wall Street or the financial media. You'll also have the tools to achieve a guaranteed income for life.

We're going to take the annuity apart, dissect it, so you'll get to know each and every section of it. Before you buy an annuity from an advisor, exchange an annuity, or take a distribution, you will benefit from reading this book. I hear advisors and brokers toss around the term *peace of mind.* After you've read this book and understand what you can do using variable annuities to guarantee your financial future, you will experience the meaning of that phrase. The single greatest obstacle our generation faces to reaching peace of mind is securing money we'll need in the future when our earning years are long over.

I hope you enjoy reading this book as much as I did writing it. I find great pleasure in creating a road map that will improve the lives of those who take the time to read and implement the following strategies. Best of luck!

ACKNOWLEDGMENTS

For the last 10 years, I have been fortunate to meet thousands of consumers, advisors, and executives with financial services companies. I have always believed that you can learn a tremendous amount from every person you meet. I would like to think that this book is an accumulation of the knowledge I have gathered from each of these people.

I want to especially thank a few people who have made it possible for me to be in the position of sharing with you information that can make a tremendous difference in your life. I have to start with my family. Writing a book is a long and strenuous process. During the final weeks of preparation, before sending the manuscript to McGraw-Hill for publication, I worked day and night. I sincerely appreciate my wife Lisa and my daughter Kendall's patience and support throughout the process.

In addition to my family, I want to thank the people I work with at AEGON Financial Services Group, Inc., Advisor Resources. I am very lucky to be surrounded by such a bright group of people who always have the consumer's best interest in mind. Special thanks go to Brad Michels, Kevin Brever, Kristin Rubino, Richard Passafiume, Linda Lyons, Sherry Stanfield, Michael Waldridge, Beth Jones, Chuck Bandy, Ann Johnson,

Greg McCarty, Deana Riley, Scott Sullivan, Jeff Schriner, Damon Yorke, Bill Evans, Rob Lotze, Brock Lansdale, and Ken Hanson. I also want to thank AEGON and particularly Larry Norman for understanding the value of this book.

I would like to thank the people I look to as mentors. People like Dan Wheeler, John Bowen, and Gene Dongieux have taught me everything I know about the advisor business and the benefits to you, the consumer.

Finally, a special thanks to Larry Chambers, my writing coach, for dealing with my panic attacks at 3 a.m. when I felt as though the book would never be finished.

You all have made a significant impact on my life and, with your help, I hope to make a significant impact on many others.

PART ONE

Getting Acquainted with Annuities

CHAPTER 1

What Are Variable Annuities?

Variable annuities were first introduced in 1952 by the College Retirement Equities Fund (CREF) to supplement a fixed-dollar annuity in financing retirement pensions. Today, variable annuities are used to supplement retirement programs such as 401(k) plans, defined benefit programs, and Social Security.

Variable annuities are often called "mutual funds with an insurance wrapper." A variable annuity combines the best aspects of a traditional *fixed* annuity (tax deferral, insurance protection for beneficiaries, tax-timing controlled-income options) with the benefits of traditional mutual fund portfolios (flexibility in selecting how to invest funds, the potential for higher investment returns).

Already an integral element of many retirement strategies that combine employee-sponsored retirement savings programs and Social Security benefits, the variable annuity market is exploding. Investment planners and advisors are recognizing variable annuities as an appropriate long-term vehicle for accumulating wealth in equities on a tax-deferred basis. In 1997, assets in annuities totaled more than $800 billion.

Variable annuity investors control their contract options. They dictate the amount, frequency, and regularity of their contributions, how their contributions are invested, and when the money is disbursed. The investor pays a premium to the insurance company, which then buys *accumulation units*, similar to mutual fund shares, in an investment fund. The IRS imposes no limits on the annual nonsheltered amount an individual may contribute to a variable annuity funded with after-tax dollars. In other words, you can put in as much money as you can afford. This is particularly important when it comes to supplementing retirement assets beyond the annual tax-free contribution limitation.

The variable annuity investor directs those funds in sub-account portfolios consisting of either stocks, bonds, or cash money-market funds. Diverse investment options make it possible to structure an investment portfolio to meet a variety of needs, goals, and risk tolerances. These investments may be managed by a mutual fund company or by the insurance company. With the important advantage of tax-free rebalancing, investors can adjust their portfolios at any time. This allows an investor's advisor to carefully plan and manage the asset allocation strategy based on changing needs or market conditions without having to worry about generating current tax.

Unlike a mutual fund, an annuity does not pay out earnings or distribute any capital gains, so these are compounded on a tax-deferred basis. The ability to reallocate assets without current tax ramifications, combined with the tax-deferred compounding of potential earnings, makes variable annuities a highly competitive investment vehicle.

A variable annuity's rate of return is not guaranteed but, rather, is determined by the performance of the investments selected. As the value of the stocks in the portfolio varies, each unit will be worth more or less. Today's variable annuity managers, along with their affiliate mutual fund managers, seek diversification, consistent performance, and competitive returns by maximizing a portfolio's return and also minimizing the level of risk. Variable annuity investments are often balanced by investing a percentage of assets in the fixed-income annuity option to provide a less volatile investment return. These fixed annuity investments tend to smooth out extreme fluctuations; investors won't profit as much from a good year in the market with such an annuity, but neither will they suffer as much loss of income during a bad year.

Payouts from variable annuities reflect the investment experience of the underlying portfolios. The amount of variable payments is not guaranteed or fixed and may decline in periods of market decline. However, if the annuitant dies during the accumulation phase (that is, prior to receiving payments from the annuity), the investor's designated beneficiary is guaranteed to receive the greater of the account's accumulated value or the full amount invested less any withdrawals and applicable premium taxes. Some annuities also offer *enhanced death benefits,* such as options that would enable a client to receive a step up every six years until age 81 to lock in gains. (The step-up feature locks in growth at designated policy anniversaries, i.e., 6 years.) Also, in most states, this built-in benefit generally bypasses the delays and costs of probate.

There is no specified age (except in Pennsylvania and New York) at which payments must begin from a variable annuity funded with after-tax dollars. When withdrawals do begin, only the amounts withdrawn that represent a gain are taxed at ordinary tax rates, while the remainder of the account value can continue to grow tax-deferred. However, if the investor takes funds from the annuity before age $59\frac{1}{2}$, there is the additional 10 percent IRS penalty on the withdrawal of any gain.

Variable annuities provide a variety of guaranteed payment options to the *annuitant,* that is, the designated recipient of the income payout:

- Lifetime income: The entire account value is converted to a monthly income stream guaranteed for as long as the annuitant lives.
- Lifetime income with period certain: Income stream is guaranteed for a specified number of years or for as long as the annuitant lives, whichever is longer.
- Refund life annuity: The entire account value is converted to a monthly income stream guaranteed for as long as the annuitant lives. If the annuitant dies prior to the principal amount being annuitized, the balance is paid to the beneficiary.
- Joint and survivor: Income stream is guaranteed for as long as either annuitant lives (for example, you or your spouse).
- Fixed period certain: The entire account value is fully paid out during a specified period of time.
- Fixed amount annuity: Equal periodic installments are withdrawn until the account balance is exhausted.

The lifetime guaranteed income payout option insures investors against the danger of outliving their money and also offers continued tax control. Part of each payment comes from principal and part from earned interest. Taxes are only assessed on the portion of each payment that comes from earned interest (except with qualified contracts). Once a guaranteed income option is elected, the investor usually cannot withdraw money or surrender his or her contract.

Most variable annuities offer a free annual withdrawal provision that gives the investor access of up to 10 percent of the annuity value annually without paying any surrender charges. Any distributions in excess of that 10 percent are subject to the surrender charges. No-load variable annuities that do not impose a surrender charge are 100 percent liquid but, like all annuities, may be subject to a 10 percent federal penalty for withdrawal of gain prior to age 59½.

Despite their inherent advantages, all variable annuities are *not* created equal. They can vary widely in terms of costs and available investment options. Because of their insurance benefits, variable annuities generally cost more than traditional taxable investments, such as mutual funds. There may be front-end charges (loads), management fees, and sometimes back-end surrender charges for early withdrawals from the policy. These charges and the length of time they apply to the policy vary widely across the industry. The average policy probably has a 6 to 7 percent first-year surrender charge that declines one percentage point per year. Some have "rolling surrender charges," which means that each investment you make has a new surrender charge schedule; for example, if you invest $1000 every year, each $1000 contribution has a new surrender charge schedule. I would avoid these if possible.

In addition to portfolio management fees, variable annuities charge a fee to cover the issuing insurance company's administrative costs and mortality and expense (M&E) charges. According to the 1997 Morningstar benchmarks, annual M&E charges for the current industry average are around 1.3 percent and are increasing.

The higher the overall costs, the longer it takes for the benefit of tax deferral to compensate for those costs. A no-sales-load, low-cost variable annuity can help shorten that breakeven holding period. In general, variable annuities are designed to be held as long-term investment vehicles, so a breakeven of 10 to 15 years may be affordable for those investors with that type of time frame. Remember, time horizon is not measured by when you will retire; it is measured according to the time you would need to start withdrawals. Income distributions from a variable annuity are best used to supplement conventional retirement benefits or as a reserve until other payouts are exhausted.

The variable annuity appears to be the answer to the shortfall retirement problems of longer life expectancies and longer retirement periods. Current trends are leading to drastic and alarming reductions in expected pension benefits, as both corporations and government are getting out of the retirement benefits business.

Let's next discuss variable annuity sub-accounts, what they are, and how they work—the subject of Chapter 2.

What Is a Sub-Account?

A sub-account is the mutual fund portfolio held inside a variable annuity.

Variable annuities offer anywhere from 5 to 35 sub-account investment options. Mutual fund account managers select individual securities inside the sub-accounts; the investor then selects the most appropriate sub-account based on the security selection for his or her portfolio. If this sounds exactly like a mutual fund, that's because it is. The same mutual funds (or "clones," as they are called) tend to have the same managers inside variable annuity sub-accounts, so the same criteria exist for choosing a mutual fund as for choosing a sub-account—and the same benefits also exist, such as professional money management, convenience, economies of scale, and diversification. Sub-account exchanges do not create taxable events and do not entail sales or transfer charges. Most companies do set limits on the number of annual exchanges (usually a maximum of 12) before a transfer fee is charged.

The variable annuity, however, gives the added benefit of tax-deferred wealth accumulation. Sub-accounts usually include a list of the primary investment objectives, and it's relatively easy to determine what the fees are applied for. Sub-accounts must specify the primary group of securities held and the issuing insurance or mutual fund company.

THE INVESTMENT FLOW OF A SUB-ACCOUNT

All investment funds flow through the insurance company into the various sub-accounts, depending on those chosen by the investor or investment advisor.

Each sub-account has a specific investment objective. Combined with other sub-accounts, this gives the investor a chance for diversification and the ability to select different portfolios to meet asset allocation and diversification needs. Sub-account managers purchase stocks, bonds, or cash, which is valued daily as an accumulation unit, another name for fund share price of the mutual fund.

Accumulation units—shares—are purchased by the contract owner at accumulation unit value (AUV), which is very similar to the mutual fund equivalent known as net asset value (NAV), without commissions, in full and fractional units.

TYPES OF SUB-ACCOUNTS

Sub-accounts may be divided into several broad categories: asset classes seeking aggressive growth, asset classes seeking more stable growth, asset classes seeking low volatility utilizing fixed-income bonds, a combination of these, and asset classes featuring money market rates. Inside each of these classes, categories are further broken down.

Fixed-income accounts are established to decrease risk for those in need of meeting current income requirements. Fixed-income sub-accounts include government agencies, corporate rate bonds, high-yield, foreign (or international) government corporate bonds, and certain-fixed income choices.

Equity or stock investing would be in funds for growth of principal. Since variable annuities are long-term investments, the equity sub-accounts will be most important to review.

Other asset classes could include cash and cash equivalents, which would be more short-term. Table 2.1 illustrates the investment options available in a variable annuity offered to consumers through investment advisors. I have illustrated in the last column the types of asset class that are represented. Remember, asset classes are groups of stocks with similar attributes that behave similarly during changing economic conditions.

You still may have questions about sub-accounts and mutual funds, how they work, and what makes up a mutual fund. The next chapter will address these questions. As you read it, think of a mutual fund and a sub-account inside the variable annuity as being the same thing. Although they are kept separate, and the fund within each cannot be commingled, for ease of understanding how a sub-account works, we will look at its predecessor, the mutual fund.

TABLE 2.1

Sub-Accounts

Portfolio	Objective	Type of Investment	Asset Class Represented
Small Cap Value	Capital appreciation	Equity securities of small U.S. and foreign companies	U.S. Small Cap
Enhanced Index	Total return modestly in excess of the performance of the S&P 500 Index	Primarily equity investments of large- and medium-sized U.S. companies	U.S. Large Cap
Domestic Blue Chip	Primarily long-term growth of capital; secondarily providing income	Common stocks of "blue-chip" companies	U.S. Large Cap
Utility Fund	High current income & moderate capital appreciation	Equity & debt securities of utility companies	Energy
Money fund	Current income with stability of principal and liquidity	High-quality money market instruments	Cash
High-Yield income Bond Fund	High current income and overall total return	Lower-rated fixed-income securities	High-Yield Fixed Income

Continued

TABLE 2.1

Concluded

Portfolio	Objective	Type of Investment	Asset Class Represented
U.S. Government Securities	Current income	U.S. government securities	Short-Term Fixed Income
Emerging Markets	Capital appreciation	Equity securities of companies in countries having emerging markets	Emerging Markets
Growth Equity	Capital appreciation	Primarily equity securities of domestic companies	U.S. Large Cap
Domestic Small Cap	Capital appreciation	Primarily common stocks, convertibles, and other equity-type securities with emphasis on small company stocks	U.S. Small Cap
International Fund	Capital growth	Primarily equity securities of companies located outside the U.S.	International Large Cap
Value Fund	Primarily long-term capital apppreciation; secondarily current income	Equity securities of medium- to large-sized companies, primarily in the U.S.	U.S. Large Cap Value
International Small Cap	Long-term capital appreciation	Primarily equity securities of small- and medium-sized foreign companies	International Small Cap
International Equity	Capital appreciation	Equity securities of non-U.S. companies	International Large Cap
Small Company Growth	Capital growth	Equity securities of small-sized U.S. companies	U.S. Small Cap

CHAPTER 3

Comparing Mutual Funds and Sub-Accounts

Let's look even deeper at what sub-accounts are by reviewing a detailed description of what mutual funds are. (If you are familiar with mutual funds and how they are structured, you may choose to skip this section.)

Think of a mutual fund as a financial intermediary that makes investments on your behalf. The mutual fund pools all its investors' funds together and buys stocks, bonds, or other assets on behalf of the group as a whole. Each investor receives a certificate of ownership and a regular statement of his or her account, indicating the value of the shares of the total investment pool. This pool of money is represented by mutual fund shares.

A mutual fund, in other words, is an investment company that makes investments on behalf of its participants who share common financial goals. The fund pools your money with others who have different amounts to invest.

Mutual funds continually issue new shares of the fund for sale to the public. The number of shares and the price are directly related to the value of the securities the mutual fund holds. A fund's share price can change from day to day, depending on the daily value of its underlying securities. To simplify your thinking: The main difference at this point between the mutual fund and the sub-account is that an insurance company charges an additional fee on a sub-account, and the tax usually paid on a mutual fund gain is deferred with a sub-account until you make withdrawals.

The main reasons people invest in mutual funds are convenience, accessing professional knowledge, and the opportunity to earn higher returns through a combination of growth and reinvestment of dividends. To understand why mutual funds are so popular, let's examine the main benefits of owning mutual funds and just how mutual funds work.

HOW MUTUAL FUNDS AND SUB-ACCOUNTS WORK

The manager of the mutual fund uses the pool of capital to buy a variety of stocks, bonds, or money-market instruments based on the advertised financial objectives of the fund. The mutual fund manager uses the investment objectives as a guide when choosing investments. These objectives cover a wide range. Some follow aggressive policies, involving greater risk in search of higher returns. Others seek current income and little risk.

When you purchase mutual fund shares, you pay *net asset value*, which is the value of the fund's total investment minus any debt, divided by the number of outstanding shares. For example, if the fund's investment value is $26,000, it has no debt, and there are 1000 shares outstanding, the net asset value (NAV) would be $26 per share. In a regular mutual fund, which includes thousands and often millions of shares, the NAV is calculated on a daily basis, with values moving up or down along with the stock or bond markets. The NAV is not a fixed figure because it must reflect the daily change in the price of the securities in the fund's portfolio. In contrast, a variable annuity issues shares at accumulation unit value (AUV). The only difference between the two is that inside a mutual fund you will sometimes pay higher than the NAV for shares that have front-end commissions, and in annuities this is not an option.

The biggest mistake that novice investors make when buying mutual funds is looking first (and sometimes only) at the prior performance of the fund or paying too much attention to the current bond fund yield. Fund costs are an important factor in the return that you earn from a mutual fund. Fees are deducted from your investment. All other things being equal, high fees and other charges depress your returns.

Costs

By keeping a careful eye on costs, you put more money to work for you in your investment. It's simply common sense that lower expenses generally translate into higher overall returns. The goal of the smart investor is to keep his or her acquisition costs as low as possible. As mentioned earlier, looking only at the prior performance of the fund is a big mistake. After you've examined the fund's performance and its objectives, you should look at what this fund will cost you. There are four basic kinds of costs: sales charges, asset management fees, operating expenses, and transaction charges.

Sales Charges

Sales charges (or loads) are commissions paid on the sale of mutual funds. All commissions used to be charged up front, but that's changed. There are now several ways that mutual fund companies charge fees.

With A-share mutual funds you pay a load that is subtracted from the initial mutual fund investment (see Table 3.1). A no-load fund does not have this charge, although other fees or service charges may be buried in its cost structure. One common charge you will find in a no-load fund is a 12b-1 fee. These are fees that are charged to the consumer to pay for the marketing costs of the mutual fund. This can include "trail" commissions to brokers. Don't be misled: Most mutual funds have a sales charge consisting of front-end, back-end, or 12b-1 fees.

B-share mutual funds have no front-end sales charges but a higher internal cost. If you decide to redeem your shares early, usually within the first five years, you pay a surrender charge. A customer who redeems shares in the first year of ownership would typically pay a 5 percent sales charge. The charge would drop by an equal amount each year; after six years, the shares would be redeemed without further charge.This is very similar to annuity investing. For large purchases, you should never purchase B-share mutual funds. There are less than ethical brokers out there who will tell you it is better to invest in B-shares since you will not pay an up-front charge. The bottom line is that if you invest a large amount, you will get a breakpoint inside an A-share mutual fund and your annual costs will be lower.

TABLE 3.1

Commission Schedule for a Typical Mutual Fund

	Sales Commission as a Percentage of:	
Purchase Amount (A-shares)	Public Offering	Net Amount Invested
Less than $50,000	5.00%	5.26%
$50,000 but less than $100,000	4.00%	4.17%
$100,000 but less than $250,000	3.00%	3.09%
$250,000 but less than $500,000	2.00%	2.04%
$500,000 but less than $1,000,000	1.00%	1.01%
$1,000,000 or more	0.00%	0.00%

Class C shares typically have even higher internal expenses and pay the selling broker up to 1 percent per year based on assets. This fee comes directly from your investment performance. C-shares may have no up-front fee, possibly a 1 percent deferred sales charge in year one (sometimes longer), and higher annual expenses (up to 1 percent extra per year).

In Table 3.1 you will notice that the offering price is different from the net amount invested. The offering price, also known as the ask price, is greater than the fund's NAV (net asset value). The NAV is identified as the amount per share you would receive if you sold your shares.

No-load mutual funds do *not* mean *no cost*. Some no-load funds charge a redemption fee of 1 to 2 percent of the net asset value of the shares to cover expenses incurred mainly by advertising and to eliminate the advantage of frequent trading. Buying a no-load mutual fund is like doing your own plumbing work. If you know what you're doing, you can save money; but if you don't have the required time and expertise, you can make a serious mistake. I highly recommend working with an investment advisor who can offer institutional no-load funds. Another important fact to remember is that when you call the toll-free number of a mutual fund company with a question, you are serviced by an employee of the mutual fund company and the advice you receive may be biased. An independent investment advisor, on the other hand, is more likely to give an unbiased reply.

A qualified investment advisor does much more than simply select a couple of mutual funds for a customer. He or she takes the short- and long-term needs, concerns, and objectives of the customer into account and builds a financial plan. Investors who are truly devoted to learning about financial matters and who follow financial news, reading enough to keep themselves well informed, may be able to do this for themselves, but most investors are not in this category and are well advised to seek professional guidance for their investments.

Asset Management Fees

Asset management fees, the fees paid to the sub-account manager for managing sub-account assets, are debited from the AUV and are reflected in your investment return. Because of the large amounts of assets under management, insurance and investment companies are able to offer *economies of scale,* or competitive fee schedules, to their customers. The management fees charged depend on the complexity of the asset management demands. Foreign equity management requires substantially more research, specialized implementation, and transaction costs than the management of a U.S. government bond fund, and the fees will reflect those differences. Equity sub-account fees are usually higher than bond sub-account fees.

Fee comparisons are particularly important. Every dollar charged comes directly from the performance of the sub-account. Remember to compare the proverbial apples to apples: in this case, similar equities to equities sub-accounts and similar bonds to bonds sub-accounts (see Table 3.2).

Operating Expenses

Fees pay for the operational costs of running a fund. These costs can include employees' salaries, marketing, servicing the toll-free phone line, printing and mailing published materials, computers for tracking investments and account balances, accounting fees, and so on. A fund's operating expenses are quoted as a percentage of

TABLE 3.2

Fee Comparisons: Various Sub-Accounts

Sub-account	Annual Performance	Management Fees	Net Performance
Foreign Equities	12.50%	1.25%	11.25%
U.S. Large Cap	12.50%	1.00%	11.50%
U.S. Small Cap	13.00%	1.20%	11.8%
Investment-grade Bonds	7.80%	0.65%	7.15%
High-yield Bonds	9.25%	0.75%	8.50%
Foreign Bonds	9.25%	0.90%	8.35%

your investment; the percentage represents an annual fee or charge. You can find this number in a fund's prospectus in a section entitled "Total Fund Operating Expenses" or "Other Expenses."

A mutual fund's operating expenses are normally invisible to investors because they're deducted before any return is paid, and they are automatically charged on a daily basis. Beware, though, a sub-account can have a very low management fee but have exorbitant operating expenses. A fund that frequently trades will have more wire charges, for instance, than a fund that does not.

Transaction Charges

When an individual investor places an order to buy 300 shares of a $30 stock ($9000 investment), he or she is likely to get a commission bill for about $207, or 2.3 percent of the value of the investment. Even at a discount broker, commissions are likely to cost between $81 (0.9 percent) and $108 (1.2 percent). A mutual fund, on the other hand, is more likely to be buying 30,000 to 300,000 shares at a time! Their commission costs often run in the vicinity of one-tenth of the commission you would pay at a discount broker! Your commission might have been $0.35 a share; the mutual fund could pay $0.05 a share or even less! The commission savings can (and should) mean higher returns for you as a mutual fund shareholder. There are even some managers, such as those at Dimensional Fund Advisers, who perform block trades when they want to buy a stock. Block trades are large blocks (e.g., rather than buying 1000 shares of IBM a day, these managers buy 100,000 shares at a time. When buying large blocks, one generally "bids" lower than the asking price, which often provides an immediate return. This is referred to as negative trading cost. This is very rare but can be a great benefit to investors since the negative cost is a direct improvement to your performance.

More General Information You Should Know

Dividends
Dividends and capital gains (the profits from a sale of stock) are paid in proportion to the number of mutual fund shares you own. So even if you invest a few hundred dollars, you get the same investment return per dollar as those who invest millions. Problem is, you will have to pay taxes on this even if it is reinvested. With a variable annuity you can defer those taxes until you plan to spend the money.

Prospectus and Annual Reports
Mutual fund companies produce information that can help you make decisions about mutual fund investments. Every fund must issue a prospectus. This legal document is reviewed and audited by the U.S. Securities and Exchange Commission (SEC). To most investors, much of what's written in the prospectus isn't worth the time it takes to muddle through; but I recommend doing so anyway to avoid future surprises.

Statements
Any mutual fund in which you participate will send you a year-end statement itemizing the income you've received. You should save this sheet along with other records of dividends, tax-exempt interest, and capital gains distributions, as well as records of the amounts received from the sale of shares. The advantage to investing in a variable annuity is that you do not have to keep track of anything since you will not owe any tax until you take a withdrawal.

Full-Time Professionals

When you invest in a sub-account or mutual fund, you are hiring a team of professional investment managers to make complex investment judgments and handle complicated trading, record keeping, and safekeeping responsibilities for you. People whose full-time profession is money management will sift through thousands of available investments in order to choose those that, in their judgment, are best suited to achieving the investment goals of a fund as spelled out in the fund's prospectus.

Full-time professionals select the portfolio's securities and then constantly monitor investments to determine if they continue to meet the fund's objectives. As economic conditions change, professionals may adjust the mix of the fund's investments to adopt a more aggressive or defensive posture. Having access to research analysis and computerized support, professional management can identify opportunities in the markets that the average investor may not have the expertise or access to identify.

Diversification

Diversification is one important characteristic that attracts many investors to mutual funds. The advantage of diversifying is that your savings are not unduly exposed to any one kind of risk. By owning a diverse portfolio of many stocks and/or bonds, investors can reduce the risk associated with owning any individual security.

To go it alone, you would need to invest money in at least 8 to 12 different securities in different industries to ensure that your portfolio could withstand a downturn in one or more of the investments. A mutual fund is typically invested in 25 to 100 or more securities. Proper diversification ensures that the fund receives the highest possible return at the lowest possible risk given the objectives of the fund.

Mutual funds do not escape share-price declines during major market downturns. For example, mutual funds that invested in stocks certainly declined during the October 27, 1997, market crash when the Dow Jones plunged 554.26 points. However, the most unlucky investors that month were individuals who had all of their money riding in Asian mutual funds; some fund shares plunged in price by as much as 30 to 40 percent that month. Widely diversified mutual funds were least hit.

Low Initial Investment

Each mutual fund establishes the minimum amount required to make an initial investment and the minimum amount that can be added to the fund. A majority of mutual funds have low initial minimums, some less than $1000. Annuities are similar with minimums generally being in the $5000 range.

Liquidity

One of the key advantages of mutual funds stems from the liquidity they provide. You can sell your shares at any time, and mutual funds have a "ready market" for their shares. Additionally, shareholders receive directly any dividend or interest payments earned by the fund, usually on a quarterly basis. When the fund manager sells some of the investments at a profit, the net gain is also distributed, but net losses are retained by the fund. Inside the mutual fund, when the dividends or capital gains are disbursed, the NAV is reduced by the disbursement. Inside the variable annuity, the AUV is unchanged by dividend and capital gains disbursements since they are not sent directly to shareholders who would consequently have to pay tax. The annuity sub-account adds tremendous value in that way to the consumer. Whereas you have to be very careful not to purchase a mutual fund prior to the ex-dividend date (the date dividends are announced) when the NAV goes down, with the variable annuity, these dates are irrelevant.

Audited Performance

All mutual funds are required to disclose historical data about the fund through their prospectus, including returns earned by the fund, operating expenses and other fees, and the fund's rate of trading turnover. The SEC audits these disclosures for accuracy. Having the SEC on your side is like having a vigilant guard dog trained on the guy who's responsible for your money. Remember, all sub-accounts inside variable annuities are registered investments. This does not mean that the SEC recommends them, but it does mean the SEC has reviewed them for abuse and fraud.

Automatic Reinvestment

One of the major benefits of mutual funds is that dividends can be reinvested automatically and converted into more shares. One of the disadvantages is that you would have to pay tax on these dividends even if you did not use them. Inside the variable annuity, this is avoided. The result inside the variable annuity is a compounded investment, whereas inside the mutual fund, you have to come up with money out of pocket or redeem shares to pay this tax. In addition, investors who own individual stocks or bonds outside the variable annuity program must continually decide how to reinvest the stream of dividends and interest they receive. Take the typical example of a $10,000 U.S. Treasury bond that pays $300 interest every six months (or 6 percent a year). You can't buy a $300 Treasury bond, so the interest is usually left to accrue in a money market brokerage account. This delay, possibly caused by the inability to reinvest, keeps savers from experiencing the magic of compounding interest.

Switching

Switching, or exchange privilege, is offered by most mutual funds through so-called family or umbrella plans. Switching from one sub-account to another accommodates changes in investment goals, as well as changes in the market and the economy. Again, in mutual funds this switching creates taxable implications. When you redeem the Federated Growth and Income Fund and buy the Federated New York Municipal Bond Fund, for example, you have to pay taxes on the gains you had earned inside the fund you sold. Inside the variable annuity, those gains are deferred until you decide to withdraw funds from the annuity. This is a critical differentiation since new funds are constantly being created that you may want to add to your portfolio. If you own mutual funds and decide you want to sell existing shares of one fund to buy the other, you have to weigh the disadvantage of having to pay tax on the shares you are selling. I have met many investors who would love to further diversify but do not, due to the potential tax implications.

In both sub-accounts and mutual funds, the managers usually maintain cash reserves for redemptions; it's easy for a fund holder to exchange his or her investment for cash or for shares in a different fund. Some people say that annuity managers need to keep less cash on hand than mutual fund managers since annuity holdings are longer-term investments. The idea that annuity holdings are less likely to be sold is generally not true; the managers do have to fear the ease of switching due to the fact that there is no tax implication. I raise this point to shift the focus away from sales gimmicks you may hear and to get you to focus on the facts.

Flexibility in Risk Level

An investor can select from among a variety of different mutual funds, finding a risk level he or she is comfortable with, and a fund with goals that match his or her own.

1. *Stock funds.* If you want your money to grow over a long period of time, funds that invest more heavily in stocks may be most appropriate.
2. *Bond funds.* If you need current income and don't want investments that fluctuate as widely as stocks in value, more conservative bond funds may be the best choice.
3. *Money market funds.* If you want to be sure that your invested principal does not drop in value because you may need your money in the short term, a money market fund or a guaranteed fixed interest investment may best fit your needs.

No Risk of Bankruptcy

A situation in which the demand for money back (liabilities) exceeds the value of a fund's investments (assets) cannot occur with a mutual fund. The value can fluctuate, but this variation doesn't lead to the failure or bankruptcy of a mutual fund company. In fact, since the Investment Company Act of 1940 was passed to regulate the mutual fund industry, no fund has ever gone under and none probably ever will.

In contrast, hundreds of banks and dozens of insurance companies have failed in the past two decades alone. Banks and insurers can fail because their liabilities can exceed their assets. When a bank makes too many loans that go sour at the same time and depositors want their money back, the bank fails. Likewise, if an insurance company makes several poor investments or underestimates the number of claims that will be made by policyholders, it too can fail. But mutual funds and sub-accounts are held in separate accounts and are not part of an insurance company's assets. Debacles like the Executive Life problems (declared

bankruptcy) in the early 1990s can be avoided by investing in the
sub-accounts of variable annuities versus the general account of
the insurance company. If you do invest in the fixed-interest accounts, make sure that the insurance company is rated highly by
all four of the major rating agencies: Moody's, Duff & Phelps,
Standard & Poor's, and A.M. Best.

Custodian Bank

A custodian, a separate organization, holds the specific securities
in which a mutual fund is invested independent of the mutual fund
company. The employment of a custodian ensures that the fund
management company can't embezzle your funds or use assets
from a better-performing fund to subsidize a poor performer.

MAJOR TYPES OF MUTUAL FUNDS

The number of mutual funds has nearly tripled since 1980. In the
current universe of approximately 8000 funds, there are portfolios
that suit most investment risk objectives. Likewise on the sub-account front, the number of options has skyrocketed. You now have
over 1500 sub-account options available. One important note: Remember to analyze the funds that are available in your annuity.
Since they may be available in other annuities, you should shop for
the lowest price. There are funds that invest in high-quality growth
stocks, or smaller aggressive growth stocks, or stocks that pay high
dividends. Mutual funds that invest in corporate and government
bonds are also available.

Most mutual funds permit customers to exchange from one
fund to another within the group for a small fee as the customers'
personal investment objectives change. Another great feature of the
variable annuity is that, inside the fund groups, you can switch
without penalty. Inside the variable annuity, you can switch from
Fidelity to Dreyfus to J.P. Morgan all free of fees and taxes.

The fund's objectives will be stated at the opening of the prospectus, indicating whether the fund emphasizes high or low risk,
stability or speculation. Funds generally fall into one of nine major
types: growth, growth and income, income, bond, money market,
tax-free, metals, foreign, and specialized. The annuity sub-accounts
will consist mostly of stock and/or bond funds. It would make no

sense to put tax-free funds like municipal bond funds inside the variable annuity since it is tax deferred and munis are tax free.

HOW A SUB-ACCOUNT WORKS INSIDE A VARIABLE ANNUITY

After you have written your check to the variable annuity, the variable annuity company sends that check on your behalf to an organization functioning as a *transfer agent.* Here your investment is recorded and processed, and the real safeguards come into play. The agent transfers the money, not to the mutual stock fund's portfolio manager (the individual or firm that makes the investment decisions, technically known as the investment advisor), but to a *custodian bank.*

Once that custodian bank receives the money, it notifies the mutual fund that new money is available for investment. The fund manager checks a daily account balance sheet and *new moneys* are invested according to the mutual fund's investment policy.

The Investment Company Act of 1940 required independent custody for each mutual fund's assets. This has turned out to be the key provision that has sheltered the industry from potential trouble for more than half a century. Independent custody means a mutual fund's parent company can go belly-up without any loss to the fund's shareholders, because their assets are held apart from other funds and apart from the parent fund.

Contrast this business structure with the far less restrictive setup between, say, individual investors and a real estate promoter, or investors and a stockbroker who may have direct access to his clients' accounts. In any number of notorious incidents, individuals in such a position have taken the money and run.

The limited partnership of the 1970s and 1980s was an excellent example of a poor business structure. During those years, many unregulated and unregistered limited partnerships were formed and investors sent their money directly to the limited partnership company. An unscrupulous promoter could simply write himself a check. Therefore, financial scandals were numerous.

A money manager of a mutual fund has no direct access to his investors' cash. The fund manager only decides how to invest shareholders' money. The custodian who controls the underlying securities allows them to be traded or exchanged with other institutional investors only after getting proper documentation from the manager. The upshot of independent custody is that it's very hard for a fund manager to use the money for his own purposes.

The Investment Company Act adds other layers of investor protection as well. Independent accountants must regularly audit every fund; a fund's board of directors, modern-day trustees, negotiate prudent contract terms with the fund's service providers and generally oversee the operation; and the SEC has the power to inspect funds and bring enforcement action against those that break the rules. In addition, mutual fund firms have legions of compliance lawyers, essentially in-house cops paid to make sure that portfolio managers, traders, and others follow the rules.

A Code of Conduct

Under SEC rules, fund managers are required to abide by strict codes of conduct. The codes require advance reporting of personal securities transactions so that there can be no conflict of interest between a manager's personal trades and what he does with his fund's securities. A manager otherwise could "front-run" his own fund, personally buying or selling securities before the fund trades in them, to his gain and possibly the fund's loss. To avoid such potential for self-dealing—that is, favoring one fund at the expense of another—the SEC set down strict guidelines for trading securities between funds in the same company rather than on the open market.

HOW TO READ VARIABLE ANNUITY TABLES

Both *Barron's* and now *The Wall Street Journal* list annuity prices. The first column is the abbreviated form of the fund's name. Several funds listed under the same heading indicate the total funds available within a specific product.

The second column, headlined "unit price," is the accumulation unit value (AUV) price per share. The AUV is identified as the amount per share you would receive if you sold your shares. So on any given day, you can determine the value of your holdings by multiplying the AUV by the number of shares you own. Remember to take surrender charges into consideration since these are not listed in the paper.

These tables also help you to figure out what the total fees are that you pay in the sub-account. The last column lists total expenses, which consists of insurance and investment expenses.

In the following chapters, we will help you to understand more about the investment attributes of sub-accounts and mutual funds.

CHAPTER 4

Mutual Fund and Variable Annuity Investments

When you have fully funded the contribution limits of your qualified retirement plan (IRA, 401k, or KEOGH), how can you further capitalize your retirement assets? There are generally two options: (1) taxable accounts such as CDs, mutual funds, stocks (if traded), and bonds, or (2) tax-deferred vehicles, such as fixed and/or variable annuities.

Figure 4.1 demonstrates how a $100,000 investment in a tax-deferred vehicle (fixed annuity) with a 12 percent return within a 33 percent tax bracket compares to a taxable investment (CD) with an 8 percent net after-tax return. When comparing CDs to fixed annuities with the same rate of return, the "Rule of 72" (shorthand for figuring compounding) is the simplest way to assess the difference in yield. The rule is to divide the number 72 by the compound interest rate you have chosen. The result is the number of years it takes your money to double.

The figure shows that the investment in the tax-deferred vehicle doubles every 6 years (72/12=6), while the taxable investment doubles only every 9 years (72/8=9). At the end of 18 years, the net value after tax (33 percent) on the fixed annuity would be $533,333—or $133,333 higher than the CD. If you project this out to 36 years, the net after-tax advantage of the tax-deferred investment becomes a staggering $2,666,666.

FIGURE 4.1

The Value of Computing

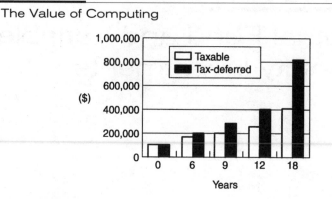

The rule of 72.

The Rule of 72 is not as easily applied when comparing mutual funds to variable annuities due to the complex nature of both investment vehicles. For instance, in most mutual funds—with the exception of fixed-income funds, hedge funds, and very high turnover equity funds—there is a portion of the return that is tax-deferred, or potentially taxed at a lower tax rate than in the tax-deferred vehicle. Thus, the mutual fund return will be subject to taxes at ordinary, as well as capital gains, rates, which range from 20 to 28 percent for those in a greater than 15 percent federal tax bracket. The portion of the distribution from a variable annuity that exceeds the contribution is taxed at ordinary income tax rates (up to 39.6 percent federal).

In Figure 4.2, we compare how a $100,000 investment within a 31 percent marginal tax bracket and a 5 percent state tax rate grows in the following two investment options:

- A mutual fund returning a gross 12 percent, with 30 percent of the annual return subject to taxation at ordinary rates (31 percent) and half of the remaining return subject to long-term capital gains rates (20 percent). The other half of the remaining return will be tax-deferred and, at distribution, taxed at the 20 percent rate. Management fees are 75 basis points or 0.75 percent.

- A variable annuity returning 12 percent tax-deferred with an insurance cost of 65 basis points or 0.65 percent and

FIGURE 4.2

Accumulation Period (30 Percent Dividend)

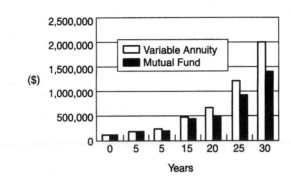

The accumulation period (30 percent dividends) between variable annuities and mutual funds.

equal management fees of 75 basis points. Upon distribution, all of the gain would be subject to ordinary income tax rates.

If, in the worst case, you were to redeem 100 percent of your investment after 30 years, the value of the variable annuity would be $104,000 greater than the mutual fund. It is important to note that although the mutual fund return is not fully taxed each year and a portion will be taxed at a potentially lower capital gains rate, the variable annuity still has more net value.

Figures 4.3, 4.4, and 4.5 illustrate the difference that utilizing a more actively managed fund will have on the accumulation value and breakeven analysis. According to a Price Waterhouse study commissioned by the National Association of Variable Annuities, an average growth mutual fund has nearly half of the return paid out as ordinary income each year, with half of the balance being subject to capital gains tax on an annual basis. There is a significant difference when you compare 50 percent versus the earlier, more conservative approach of only using 30 percent of the return paid out as ordinary income.

In this situation, using 50 percent dividends versus the 30 percent dividends of the mutual funds, the NAT—net after tax—

FIGURE 4.3

Net After-Tax Value (30 Percent Dividend)

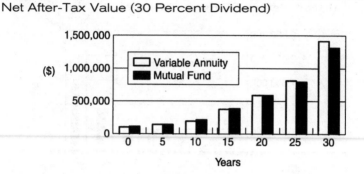

The net after-tax value (30 percent dividends) between variable annuities and mutual funds.

FIGURE 4.4

Accumulation Period (50 Percent Dividend)

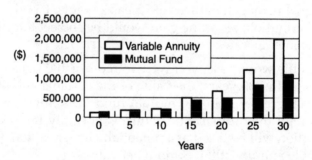

The accumulation period (50 percent dividends) between variable annuities and mutual funds.

value of the variable annuity would be over $200,000 greater. As you can see, depending on the input variables, there are dramatic differences in the investment value of an annuity compared to mutual funds. I highly recommend doing an individual analysis with an advisor using AdvisorSoft to see if an annuity is a better long-term investment for your non-qualified dollars.

In the next chapter, the most suitable uses of variable annuities will be discussed.

FIGURE 4.5

Net After-Tax Value (50% Dividend)

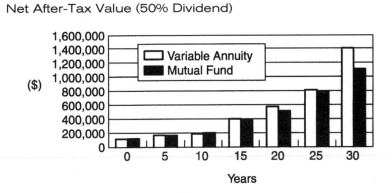

The accumulation period (50 percent dividends and net after-tax value) between variable annuities and mutual funds.

CHAPTER 5

Suitable Uses of
Variable Annuities

I have heard investors and investment advisors say something like, "I have seen the numbers and read the articles in magazines, but I still don't know just who should invest in annuities." This chapter will list what I think are the uses of annuities. Not everyone will agree with this list. Most will say I am leaving out half of the market, and they may be correct. When you look at the fact that there is close to $500 billion in variable annuities and half of that is invested with qualified funds, I have to wonder about the decisions made by the sellers. I do not believe that all qualified money inside annuities is inappropriate, as I will discuss, but I do believe that probably half of the $400 billion of qualified money inside variable annuities is inappropriately invested.

My top six list of suitable uses for variable annuities are:

1. As nonqualified systematic savings after qualified plan needs have been met
2. As lump-sum alternatives to investments in CDs or high-turnover mutual funds
3. For greater diversification potential for small IRAs
4. In certain states, to take full advantage of asset protection
5. As a funding vehicle for NIMCRUTs (Net Income with Makeup Charitable Remainder Trusts)
6. To improve a client's existing annuity or life insurance investments

I will now explain in detail why I believe that these are viable uses of variable annuities.

NONQUALIFIED SYSTEMATIC SAVINGS

Once you have met your qualified plan funding limits, which for affluent investors happens pretty quickly, you have a decision to make as to where you will invest additional funds. You can invest in one of a hundred different options, but for the long-term dollars, the variable annuity makes the most sense. If you have less than 10 years to invest, use mutual funds; if you have 10 years or more, use the variable annuity. The fact is that if you have two investments and one is taxable, that one will accumulate less funds than the tax-deferred investment. Time allows the tax deferral to overcome the negative attributes of an annuity, such as higher cost and potentially higher taxation at withdrawal. I say "potentially" because, although we know that ordinary rates are for the most part higher than capital gains rates, according to a 1997 Price Waterhouse study of annuities and mutual funds, the majority of your mutual fund investment return will likely be subject to ordinary income rates anyway.

LUMP-SUM ALTERNATIVES

Investments in CDs, bond mutual funds, and high-turnover equity mutual funds have one thing in common. All, or at least the majority, of the investment return each year will be taxable to you at ordinary income tax rates. The real question here is: If you currently have investment dollars in these types of accounts and you are not using the investment income for living expenses, why are you paying taxes on it? You would be much better off deferring those taxes until you need the income. This one is a no-brainer since even the breakevens are in single digits. You would be better off in the annuity, despite the additional cost, after just a few short years.

GREATER DIVERSIFICATION POTENTIAL

All right, I said that I did not believe in annuity investments inside of qualified plans. The tax-deferred annuity has a cost for the tax deferral, and you do not need that benefit in a qualified plan. Let's think for a minute about why you would now want a tax-deferred vehicle inside a tax-deferred plan. The variable annuity gives you the ability to invest in as many funds as you would like, most with $100 minimums inside one contract. Therefore, you can diversify your holdings even if your investment is small. It is very possible that the added degree of diversification would more than make up for the additional insurance expense.

Another reason may be that you are working with an investment advisor. If he or she clears through Schwab or Fidelity, for example, you usually incur transaction fees for any switches or investments that take place. Inside the annuity, you are typically not charged. If you have $50,000 in an IRA and you or your advisor makes eight switches each year at $35/switch, that would cost 56 basis points, almost the same charge as some of the low-cost no-load variable annuities. If you make more switches or have a lower account balance, the cost would be even higher. Therefore, the annuity may be a lower-cost alternative.

ASSET PROTECTION

What is asset protection? Well, in certain states—Arkansas, Florida, Michigan, New York, North Dakota, Ohio, Oklahoma, and Texas—annuities are a shelter from creditors. If you are a physician in Florida and you have a fear of someday being sued for malpractice, an annuity may be a great savings tool. I recommend consulting a tax advisor in your area to learn more about annuities and asset protection. It could be the best place to put money if you work in an economically hazardous occupation.

A FUNDING VEHICLE FOR NIMCRUTS

I have probably lost most everyone here by using the word "NIM-CRUT." When I first used it at a meeting a couple of years ago, everyone looked at me as if I was speaking German. NIMCRUT stands for a Net Income with Makeup Charitable Remainder Uni-Trust. It is a mouthful, but for those charitably inclined, it can be a great tool for leaving a legacy while enjoying personal financial benefit. The NIMCRUT, very simply, is a charitable trust that is most commonly funded with a highly appreciated asset. The asset is then sold within the trust without tax implications. If you are looking for a way to sell a stock without paying the gains, this may be a solution. You receive an income tax deduction for the gift based on several factors, such as age or income rate designation.

The annuity is such a great funding tool because the idea behind the NIMCRUT is to defer your income until you need it. With some investments, like mutual funds, you cannot fully defer the income since dividends and interest must be distributed. The annuity, if structured properly, can fully defer income for when you need it most. In addition, the makeup provision gives you the ability to go back and get all of the money accumulated that you had not previously received. Again, I strongly urge you to consult with a specialized estate-planning or charitable-giving attorney.

IMPROVING A CLIENT'S EXISTING INVESTMENTS

Finally, there are a lot of annuity investors around the country who have been sold a product that does not meet their needs. This also goes for many life insurance owners. The ability to do a tax-free exchange from one contract to another, annuity-to-annuity and life-to-annuity, is a great way to restructure your holdings to minimize your cost and increase the probability of higher investment returns. In the next chapter, I will discuss what to do if you already own a variable annuity.

CHAPTER 6

I Already Own a Variable Annuity, What Do I Do Now?

In 1997 alone, annuity sales surpassed $80 billion. Nearly half of these sales came from tax-free 1035 exchanges. A 1035 exchange is an IRS code that allows investors in fixed and variable annuities as well as life insurance to swap their contract for another without taxation as long as the owner, beneficiary, and other details of the contract remain the same.

These are hot resources for unscrupulous brokers looking to make a quick buck. As soon as an annuity's surrender charge is expired, you may get a call from an agent with a new and improved version of the annuity, which just happens to have a new surrender charge schedule and a big commission. The benefit to you the investor is typically low compared to the benefit to the broker. In some states like Florida, this practice of twisting is being more heavily scrutinized. The SEC is paying close attention to agents and brokers that make a living from this practice.

There is a better way. If you currently own a fixed annuity with a low renewal rate or a variable annuity that does not meet your investment portfolio needs or is too expensive, you have options that are much better than the previous scenario. Likewise, if you were sold a life insurance policy that you feel you do not need, you too can benefit from the following information.

In 1994, the annuity industry took a big step forward. Up until then, annuity clients had only one choice for a no-load variable annuity and that was offered by Vanguard. It was largely unheard of and the investment options were limited. Since 1994, more companies have created no-load variable annuities as a way for consumers to increase returns and lower costs of existing contracts. Out of the $800 billion in fixed and variable annuities, only about $4 billion is invested in these no-loads. Of that $4 billion, nearly three-quarters of the funds are with one insurance company, Providian Life and Health, a subsidiary of AEGON USA. Other entrants in the recent past include Schwab, Jack White, and T. Rowe Price. I do not include Fidelity because its contract has a five-year surrender charge schedule, therefore it is not a no-load.

Analyze the annuity you have and check the mortality cost and fund expenses against those offered by these companies. According to VARDS (Variable Annuity Research and Data Services), the lowest cost options are available from Vanguard and Dimensional Fund Advisors. Harold Evensky, in his book *Wealth Management*, mentions The Advisor's Edge offered by Providian Life and Health as an interesting annuity option. You can find phone numbers for these and other variable annuity providers in the appendix.

THE ANALYTICAL COMPARISON

A 1035 exchange has one potential drawback. If you have a surrender charge schedule remaining and you move to a new contract, you will be penalized by your existing company. A company may rebate the agent commission to offset this fee, but remember, if the fees are high and you assume a new surrender charge schedule, you probably will not benefit greatly with this move. These annuities are more of a gimmick and a way for brokers to earn commissions that otherwise would be unavailable for a few years.

In Tables 6.1 through 6.3, I present information that shows when a 1035 exchange is appropriate. I will analyze moving into a no-load variable annuity from a commission-based annuity with a surrender charge schedule remaining. We will observe how a 75 basis point difference in return and lower insurance charges may greatly impact your decision.

If the scenario in Table 6.1 described the situation of investor 1, the result of the 1035 exchange during the first 10 years, from a before-tax and after-tax value, would be as shown in Table 6.2.

TABLE 6.1

Comparison of Current and Proposed Annuity

Variables	Current Annuity	Proposed Annuity
Contributions Made to Date	$100,000	0
Current Value	$150,000	0
Gross Investment Return	10%	10%
Insurance Cost	140bps	65bps
Portfolio Fees	75bps	75bps
Surrender Charges Remaining	2, 1, 0	0
Federal and State Tax Rate of Consumer	34%	34%

TABLE 6.2

Comparison of Current and Proposed Policy Results
10 Percent Return

	Current Policy Results			Proposed Policy Results			
Year	Account Value	After-tax Value	Total Return	Account Value	After-tax Value	Total Return	Proposed Policy Advantage
1	161,548	140,563	6.29%	159,554	140,306	–6.46%	(257)
2	173,988	150,075	0.03%	173,147	149,506	–0.16%	(570)
3	187,389	159,145	1.99%	187,901	159,491	2.07%	346
4	201,824	168,914	3.01%	203,915	170,329	3.23%	1,415
5	217,373	179,438	3.65%	221,296	182,093	3.95%	2,655
6	234,123	190,775	4.09%	240,162	194,862	4.46%	4,087
7	252,167	202,986	4.42%	260,639	208,720	4.83%	5,734
8	271,603	216,141	4.67%	282,865	223,763	5.13%	7,622
9	292,540	230,311	4.88%	306,988	240,090	5.37%	9,779
10	315,093	245,575	5.05%	333,172	257,811	5.57%	12,236

TABLE 6.3

Comparison of Current and Proposed Policy Results
11 Percent Return

	Current Policy Results			Proposed Policy Results			
Year	Account Value	After-tax Value	Total Return	Account Value	After-tax Value	Total Return	Proposed Policy Advantage
1	161,548	140,563	6.29%	161,014	141,294	-5.80%	732
2	173,988	150,075	0.03%	176,331	151,661	0.55%	1,586
3	187,389	159,145	1.99%	193,109	163,016	2.81%	3,871
4	201,824	168,914	3.01%	211,486	175,453	4%	6,539
5	217,373	179,438	3.65%	231,615	189,077	4.74%	9,638
6	234,123	190,775	4.09%	253,662	203,999	5.26%	13,224
7	252,167	202,986	4.42%	277,812	220,343	5.65%	17,357
8	271,603	216,141	4.67%	304,264	238,246	5.95%	22,105
9	292,540	230,311	4.88%	333,238	257,855	6.20%	27,545
10	315,093	245,575	5.05%	364,974	279,334	6.42%	33,759

As you can see in this illustration, the client is better off by over $12,000 in the 10th year by exchanging the annuity. This of course assumes that the client received equal investment returns and that he or she assumed a 2 percent surrender charge to move the contract. The net after-tax account value of the contract for the new annuity takes about three years to be better off.

Table 6.3 shows what happens if your new policy receives a gross investment return of 11 percent rather than the previous illustration at 10 percent. The improvement is more immediate and substantial.

As you can see, the effect of 100 basis points improved return combined with 75 basis points cost difference is dramatic. If you employ the investment strategy recommendations presented later in this book—based on years of academic research by several Nobel prize winners—you improve your probability of attaining this increased investment return.

The bottom line is that you can most likely improve on your current situation. Avoid sales pitches in which your benefit is secondary to the agent's. Find an investment advisor who will help you sort through the hundreds of annuities on the market to select one that can lower your cost and increase your returns.

In the next chapter, I outline the risks associated with variable annuities.

CHAPTER 7

Risks Associated with Variable Annuities

This will be a short chapter. There are three main risks associated with variable annuities: pre-59½ distribution risk, investment risk, and tax law risk.

PRE-59½ DISTRIBUTION RISK

There is a penalty (in addition to ordinary income tax owed) on money withdrawn from a tax-deferred annuity prior to age 59½. The majority of this risk can be mitigated with proper financial planning. If you follow the four-step process of (1) establishing a liquidity fund for short-term expenses, (2) maximizing your qualified retirement plan, (3) investing in mutual funds for mid-term needs (three to seven years), and (4) investing in a variable annuity, you should be able to avoid this risk. Undoubtedly someone will have an unforeseen situation in which the annuity must be tapped for early distributions. But you cannot create a financial plan that focuses on the 1 out of 100 possibility. Invest with the belief that you will be among the 99 percent who, after following these steps, will never need an early withdrawal.

INVESTMENT RISK

All variable annuities, like mutual funds, stocks, and bonds, assume a degree of investment risk. The degree that you assume depends on the type of sub-accounts you choose to invest in. If you choose risky accounts like emerging markets or international small-cap stocks, then you should be prepared to lose money in any particular year or set of years. The risk you assume, from an investment perspective, inside a variable annuity is not higher than the risk you assume when investing in equities. The risk to your heirs, however, is reduced due to the guarantee that they will not receive anything less than you put in. This is superior to a mutual fund, stock, bond, or any other investment.

TAX LAW RISK

I first began discussing tax law risk (the risk that the government would change the tax laws and make annuities less attractive, e.g., eliminate capital gains and the tax deferral) in the early 1990s when Congress was considering the option of eliminating the tax-deferred status of annuities. This would have been devastating to consumers and insurance companies. After that discussion ended with no action taken, the next wave of tax risk discussions centered on the capital gains issue. As I will discuss in the next chapter, this risk has been realized but to a much smaller degree than initially observed.

One must remember that annuities are long-term tax-deferred investments. During your accumulation and distribution, the tax rates will constantly fluctuate. Between 1985 and 1997, the capital gains rate changed seven times. It has ranged from the current low of 20 percent to as high as 33 percent. If you think it will remain at its current level and format for more than another four years, think again.

In the next chapter, Uncle Sam's impact on investing will be discussed further.

CHAPTER 8

Annuities after the 1997 Tax Relief Program

During accumulation variable annuities have one primary advantage over mutual funds—that's tax deferral. Gains compound unencumbered by taxes. But tax deferral comes with a cost. Variable annuities typically are much pricier than mutual funds because there's an added fee for the insurance features that are embedded into the policy. The average variable annuity has total insurance and fund expenses of 2.1 percent versus 1.4 percent for the average mutual fund. So the question remains, under the 1997 Taxpayer Relief Act, does it makes sense to put new nonqualified money into a variable annuity?

UNCLE SAM'S IMPACT

All the new tax act really does is widen the spread between the tax rates that ultimately could be levied on the returns of variable annuities and other types of investments that would be subject to long-term capital gains tax rates. In so doing, the new tax act extends the time it takes for the benefits of tax deferral to offset the increased costs (consisting of fees and tax differential) of variable annuities.

When gains are withdrawn from a variable annuity, they're taxed at individual ordinary income tax rates, which can run as high as 39.6 percent. In contrast, the IRS taxes gains from selling stocks and mutual funds held for more than 18 months at the long-term capital gains rate, which for long-term investors is as low as 20 percent (as low as 10 percent for investors in a 15 percent income tax bracket) versus the old 28 percent. The consequence is that if your tax rate during retirement exceeds 20 percent, you may end up footing a heftier tax bill in a variable annuity than in a mutual fund.

The tax law change extends the breakeven (B/E) period—how long investors must hold on to their variable annuities for the net investment returns of the annuity to be superior to that of a mutual fund. Prior to the 1997 act, the general breakeven point for investors in the 28 percent tax bracket during the accumulation phase was about 8 years. Since the new tax law, the breakeven period extends in some cases to 13 years. This is an extreme generalization because the breakeven points are contingent upon several sensitivities. Figures 8.1 and 8.2 illustrate the impact the change in capital gains tax can have on the breakeven point of an annuity.

The figures illustrate the breakeven for a mutual fund and variable annuity based on the variables in Table 8.1. In Figure 8.1, the breakeven occurs in the eighth year based on the information for composition of returns provided by the Price Waterhouse study for the National Association of Variable Annuities. This, of course, is based on the old maximum capital gains rate of 28 percent. Figure 8.2 illustrates what the breakeven would be for the new maximum capital gains rate of 20 percent.

As you can see, the breakeven at the 20 percent rate is extended to about 13 years. So what does this mean to you, the investor? What it means is that you should have a longer time horizon in which to invest. If you plan to take a 100 percent distribution of the account within 13 years, do not buy the annuity. If you plan to receive a lump sum payout from the annuity in less than 8 years, do not buy the annuity. Income options become critical here. What is interesting is that even though the breakeven is 13 years at 20 percent capital gain, if you annuitize the contract after 8 years rather than taking a lump sum withdrawal as illustrated in the B/E, you were better off purchasing the annuity due to the tax-favored income afforded during the annuitization phase. We will discuss income options at more length later in this book.

TABLE 8.1

Table of Sensitivities for Figures 8.1 and 8.2

Sensitivities	Figure 8.1	Figure 8.2
Federal Tax Rate	28%	28%
State Tax Rate	6%	6%
Maximum Cap. Gains Rate	28%	20%
Gross Rate of Return	12%	12%
Portfolio Cost	.75%	.75%
Administrative Fee	$30	$30
Insurance Cost of Annuity	.65%	.65%
Dividends and Short-Term Gains of Fund	5.625	5.625
Realized Long-Term Gains of Fund	2.8125	2.8125

FIGURE 8.1

Breakeven at 28 Percent Capital Gains Rate

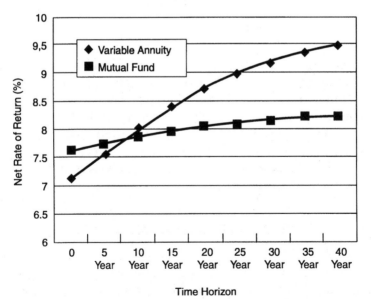

The breakeven at 28 percent capital gains rate.

FIGURE 8.2

Breakeven at 20 Percent Capital Gains Rate

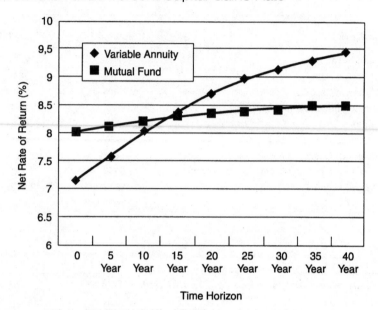

Time Horizon

The breakeven at 20 percent capital gains rate.

Under the current 20 percent maximum capital gains rate, variable annuity investors need more patience. Patient investors with a longer time horizon and those who shop around for no-load variable annuity companies will probably still be better off investing in a variable annuity than in a mutual fund. The variable annuity is not always going to be the best fit in everyone's investment strategy, but the new tax laws won't be the kiss of death to annuities, as the media predicted.

WHY THE NEW CAPITAL GAINS CUTS DON'T MAKE A BIG DIFFERENCE

The new tax changes have created a three-tiered schedule for taxing capital gains. If you hold an investment for less than 12 months and realize a gain when you sell, you will pay tax on the gain at your ordinary income tax rate (which now can be as high as 39.6 percent). If you sell a holding between 12 and 18 months after buying it, gains

TABLE 8.2

$10,000 Taxed as Ordinary Income versus Capital Gains

Gain taxed as ordinary income at 39.6%	$3,960
Gain taxed at 28% capital gains tax rate	$2,800
Gain taxed at 20% capital gains tax rate	$2,000

will be taxed at the 28 percent long-term capital gains rate. If you sell the holding after 18 months, your gains will be taxed at 20 percent. Taking maximum advantage of the new laws is based on your ability and the ability of the fund manager to invest long-term.

The reduction of the long-term capital gains tax rate to 20 percent on an 18-month holding gives you the opportunity to halve the tax penalty if you are a high-tax bracket consumer. Take, for example, a client in the 39.6 percent tax bracket whose $100,000 investment of taxable dollars returns 10 percent, producing a $10,000 gain. Investors who realize their gains within the 12 to 18-month window and pay the 28 percent capital gains tax effect a 30 percent savings over the regular income tax rate at which short-term capital gains are taxed (see Table 8.2). If they hold investments for 18 months or longer, the 20 percent tax rate reduces the amount of federal taxes by almost 50 percent versus ordinary income tax rates.

At first glance, the new tax law carries the potential to reduce tax penalties by as much as 50 percent. But this is predicated solely on not realizing the gain for a minimum of 18 months. What's not often mentioned is that institutional investors, not taxable investors, influence most stock market investing. Most mutual funds managers employ very active day-to-day short-term trading to maximize total return. This approach will take away any advantage of the new lower capital gains tax rate and still leave their taxable investors exposed up to nearly 40 percent tax.

The elimination of the "short-short" rule, which limited to 30 percent the amount of gain a mutual fund could realize from selling securities held less than 90 days, is likely to intensify this effect. It's human nature. Mutual fund managers are going to try to get the highest returns, because their jobs depend on it. They are judged quarter by quarter, not every 18 months. If they can take a profit short-term, they will—which pleases institutional investors but brings ordinary income to taxable investors. The last thing mutual fund managers are concerned about is whether they should hold a security for 12 months or 18 months. So all cases being equal, we are right back where we started before the tax act of 1997.

SO WHAT DO I DO TODAY?

Many investors ask if they should invest now in mutual funds to take advantage of the low capital gains rates, then switch to an annuity when they want to retire. If you do it that way, you will have to pay capital gains on assets accumulated before the switch to an annuity. The main benefit of the annuity is that assets can be accumulated tax-deferred, and then a switch to an income option at retirement can be made with all accumulated assets intact and free from tax.

For example, if you invest $500,000 into a variable annuity and it grows to $1 million, you do not have to cash it all in and pay tax on the $500,000 of growth at one time. If you annuitize, that million dollars will be paid to you in monthly installments from a portion of the original $500,000 and a portion of the $500,000 gain. This means that taxes are paid at a lower rate. What's even better is that you do not have to keep track of when you bought which shares and how long you held them. That's a huge advantage.

Jeff Saccacio, partner-in-charge of the West Coast Personal Financial Services Practice for Coopers & Lybrand L.L.P., says, "Assuming tax rates remain the same and that you are invested in an equity income type mutual fund, a large amount of your dividend income will be taxed at ordinary income rates. The alternative is to invest in a variable annuity product, which invests in the same type of mutual fund, but you are taxed later on the distribution."

This makes a big difference. If you get taxed now and you have high state income taxes, you're going to pay from 46 to 48 cents out of every dollar, which gets taken right off the top before reinvestment. If you invest in a variable annuity product, that 46 to 48 cents doesn't get taken out until the annuity product pays out in the future. So you get the benefit of compounding on what you otherwise would have paid in tax.

"You will accumulate more, even though you are going to pay tax on the gains in the future," says Saccacio, "This is a simple present-value calculation: that is, the present value of the future accumulation versus the present value of your earnings stream if you don't elect to use this deferral type variable annuity product. The variable annuity works if you do not need access to your money right away, plus you have an emergency cash reserve, and your goal is to accumulate funds for retirement. A variable annuity provides you with a tax shelter on an accumulation basis."

One wild card in this analysis is: What if tax rates go up in the future when you're in retirement and start taking distributions? "In that case," says Saccacio, "you would most likely be in a lower tax bracket, so you would probably still be better off using a deferral type product."

The investor who has maxed out his 401(k) and is cut off from contributing to a Roth IRA is left with the choice of after-tax contributions to his retirement plan or after-tax contributions to an IRA, both of which are extremely limited. The logical choice would be to consider a variable annuity product, which gives the sheltered growth benefits of a qualified plan.

Survey after survey reveals that building a retirement nest egg is the number one financial concern of most U.S. households. Since most people are concerned about outliving their retirement funds, accumulating money is only one side of the retirement coin. Positioning assets to provide sufficient income during retirement is equally critical.

Tax deferral offered by a variable annuity works over the long run. Maximize your variable annuity's rate of return by lowering expenses. Find variable annuities that offer high-dividend-producing mutual funds and high short-term capital gain realization portfolios. Avoid all other types of low-turnover funds or standard index funds inside the variable annuity. These should be held outside the variable annuity. Narrow your search by first finding the annuity with the lowest insurance and administrative expenses.

In the next chapter, I will discuss what I believe to be the future of annuity sales. They have been increasing rapidly; will that continue?

CHAPTER 9

The Future of Annuity Sales

There has obviously been huge overall growth in the financial industry. Up until 1988, this growth was due to the increase in sales of commission-based products, specifically mutual funds, sold by brokers. Recently, no-load products sold by investment advisors have experienced exponential growth. No-load mutual funds now make up nearly 50 percent of all financial products sold.

It is my opinion that investment advisors should be striving to be on the forefront of the upcoming growth in no-load annuities. Just as no-load mutual funds have grown to make huge sense within an advisor's practice, no-load annuities will soon make just as much sense or more. No-load annuities give the advisor the ability to create consistency for the client. The advisor can use low-cost solutions that are both taxable (mutual funds) and tax deferred (annuities). Let's say you are a consumer and your advisor explains that he works on a fee basis. If you understand the benefit of the asset management fee versus a commission, you acknowledge that having the advisor's income tied to your investment performance is preferable to a transaction commission. But what if, after explaining this, he then uses a commission annuity for your tax-deferred investments? Doesn't this go against everything that was explained? If you are an advisor, think about the message you send to the client. If you are a client, ask the advisor why he does not use the same compensation methodology for the annuity.

This chapter will discuss the huge growth curve that's occurring and describe the wave that's to follow in the near future. One factor involved in that growth is the current transition from commissions to fees within the industry itself. There is a definite movement from commission mutual funds to no-load mutual funds. The reason this is happening is that advisors are realizing that consumers are more interested in service and less interested in transaction salespeople who sell a product, then are not to be seen again until a new and improved version is available. Most of the time this is just a way of earning another commission. Don't get me wrong, I do not believe that most brokers are unscrupulous; in fact I think just the opposite. I believe that most financial professionals have the client's best interest at heart, but commissions and free trips to Scandinavia, Aspen, and Hawaii can easily cloud their judgment.

Another huge factor in the move to fee advice is the developing technology that allows advisors to be much more independent and efficient. With today's technology, for instance, we now have the ability to truly analyze whether a no-load annuity makes sense for a particular client. Before 1995, an advisor had to more or less guess if the annuity would increase net investment returns over mutual funds. Those days are behind us; now you, the consumer, can demand an analytical comparison from your advisor of mutual funds and annuities using software called AdvisorSoft™.

Lastly, another reason for the shift from brokers selling commission (load) mutual funds to advisors recommending no-load mutual funds (see Figure 9.1) was the drop in commission rates—from 8 percent to 4 percent. I expect that annuity commissions will also be coming down from the lofty 6 to 7 percent range in the future.

A prediction: Two other areas will follow a similar track—variable annuities sales and, in the distant future, variable life sales. Already, no-load annuities are being sold. They're not overtaking commission-based annuities by any stretch of the imagination, but the technology is getting in place to support this shift. Consumers are also becoming more aware of hidden expense charges and insurance costs. Fees for managing portfolios are beginning to make sense in this area too. With the pricing of no-load variable annuities dropping to one-half the cost of traditional commission products, consumers can now add an advisor's fee for managing their assets

FIGURE 9.1

Trend in Mutual Fund Sales

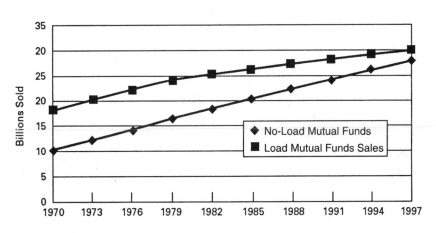

The trend in mutual fund sales: no-load versus load mutual funds.

and quarterly reviews and still keep the total cost below what they are currently paying.

Variable life salespeople, on the other hand, have not taken the leap of mass conversion to fee-based products. In this area, insurance agents receive up to 100 percent commissions with 25 percent trails (renewal commissions). There's understandably little motivation to change from 100 percent upfront to 1 percent or 2 percent based on accumulated value. Most companies handling variable life, however, are proprietary; these salespeople generally focus on a product, not a full financial plan. If you do not believe me, sit with a typical insurance agent and ask him or her which option would be better for a $2000 dollar a year investment—a mutual fund, a variable annuity, or variable life. I would predict, regardless of your situation, 7 out of 10 agents would steer you toward the variable life. Commissions can be the driving force behind the sale of life insurance and will be as long as there are sales forces that are paid as much as 100 percent commissions to sell products, not to create long-term investment solutions. If you have an insurance need, variable life may be the best investment for you. If you do not, there are much better alternatives.

We need to focus at this point on where the next (second) curve of transition to fee-based investment will be. The first upward trend is maturing rapidly on the mutual fund side. It is highly probable that the next curve will occur with annuities, based on the advent of the new no-loads. With $800 billion in the existing annuity business, only about $1 billion of that is now managed by fee-based and fee-only financial advisors.

Advisors are now able to truly examine a client's tax structure and analyze whether a product is really adding value or not. Many advisors, however, aren't even aware that these products—annuities—exist. If they do know annuities exist, they don't understand how they work. (I recommend showing this book to your advisor if he or she is not aware of no-load variable annuities.) Most advisors, even if they've been in the business 15 or 20 years, still think there's a commission involved. It's simply wrong not to offer annuities as an option in a fee-only business. Search out an investment advisor who understands annuities and uses them when suitable. (Suitability was discussed in Chapter 5.)

An advisor's main goal, after all, is to increase the probability of economic freedom for clients at retirement. It is obviously the advisor's responsibility to use the best tools available to improve that probability. If an annuity makes sense, then it's the job of the advisor to implement that tool—for the same reason that an advisor might recommend maxing out a qualified plan versus investing that money outside the plan in mutual funds. It's just a matter of making the most logical decision in the client's best interest. I don't think there's an ethical advisor who would argue with that. The problem is simply that it's not common knowledge to consider an annuity as one of the alternatives once, say, the client's qualified plan is maxed out. This has got to happen, however, because the concept is sound and it works.

The next chapter will explain the death benefit feature of the annuity.

CHAPTER 10

Annuity Death Benefit Features

How annuities are treated at death is a point of confusion for nearly everyone. If you listen to the objection I commonly hear from investment advisors, "I do not use annuities since they do not step up at death," you would never purchase an annuity. (A "step-up" is the tax-free transfer of the gross account value to heirs.) The bottom line is that annuities are not estate planning tools unless you plan to use them as a funding vehicle for charitable remainder trusts. However, the picture is not nearly as bleak as some advisors make it out to be.

The typical scenario that I hear sounds like this: "If my client owned a variable annuity and a mutual fund, when he or she died the annuity would be taxed twice and the mutual fund only once." That, my friends, is correct. But the implication here is that the annuity and the mutual fund would have equal values at the client's death. That is not likely to be the case.

If you invested in these instruments when you were 50 years old and died at the age of 80, you would have accumulated significantly more in the annuity than in the mutual fund. When your heirs pay the income tax due on the annuity, the net value is often higher than the value of the mutual fund. True, the mutual fund gets "stepped up" to the heirs, but who cares, since the value after tax is greater in the annuity. Let me prove this to you using Figure 10.1 and Table 10.1. In this scenario, we have a high-income

FIGURE 10.1

Accumulation Comparison

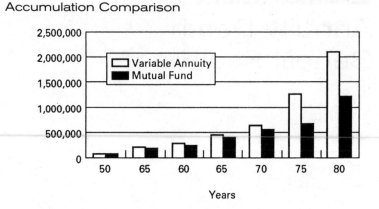

Years

Accumulation comparison between variable annuities and mutual funds.

TABLE 10.1

Comparison of Net Value to Heirs

	Variable Annuity	Mutual Fund
Initial Principal	$100,000	$100,000
Gross Total Value at Age 80	$2,008,470	$1,040,686
Income tax rate of heirs	39.6% Federal 6% State	Irrelevant
Net Value to Heirs	$1,138,209	$1,040,686

individual paying a total of 45 percent in state and federal taxes. I have used the same returns and composition of returns as in the previous figures and tables. Figure 10.1 compares the accumulated value of the variable annuity and the mutual fund.

Table 10.1 compares the value that would pass to the heirs from the variable annuity and the mutual fund. The net value of the variable annuity after taxes is still higher than the mutual fund. We have looked at only the income tax due by the heirs, not the estate tax. This gives a fair comparison of the difference in taxation since mutual funds receive a step up at death to the heirs and annuities do not. The table is alarming to most advisors.

Again, this table is based on a worst-case scenario, a lump-sum withdrawal. In this situation, your heirs would pay the highest income tax possible since the value of the annuity would push them into the maximum tax bracket. Even taking this into consideration, the variable annuity would provide $97,522 more to the heirs. Is this always the case? Of course not. There are so many variables, including estate tax considerations, that have to be considered that it is impossible to accurately predict what your heirs would receive. The object of this exercise is to prove the importance of doing your own analysis and taking with a grain of salt the things you read in the media.

Let's review the total picture regarding death benefit options, the first being the avoidance of probate.

AVOIDING PROBATE

The federal tax code sets certain distribution requirements for beneficiaries other than spouses; death proceeds may be treated in several ways (depending on the contract language, when the death takes place, and who actually dies):

1. If any owner (who is also the annuitant) dies prior to the annuity starting date, the beneficiary may
   a. retain the owner's interest in the annuity and defer distribution of the proceeds for up to five years after the owner's death; or
   b. elect to annuitize the remaining interest in the annuity over their own life expectancy (provided annuity payments begin within one year after the owner's death).
2. If any owner (who is also the annuitant) dies on or after the annuity date, but before the entire interest or contract has been distributed, the remaining interest must be distributed at least as rapidly as under the method of distribution being used at the time of the owner's death.

In some circumstances, the owner of the contract and the annuitant are not the same person. In such a contract structure, the death of the owner will result in the application of the same rules as described above. However, the death of the annuitant could result in required distributions not described here. The language in the annuity contract will address such a situation.

DISTRIBUTION OPTIONS AT DEATH

As described above, annuities provide many opportunities for flexibility in payments upon the death of the owner. Depending on whether the beneficiary is a spouse or nonspouse, the following are options that could be available:

1. Lump-sum distribution: The beneficiary withdraws the entire annuity payment in one payment.
2. Lifetime income: The beneficiary annuitizes the contract and receives an income for life.
3. Lifetime income with period certain: The beneficiary annuitizes the contract and receives an income for life and a guarantee that a certain number of payments will be made even if he or she dies prematurely.
4. Systematic withdrawals: The beneficiary determines his or her distribution needs in systematic withdrawals without annuitizing the contract.
5. No withdrawals: The beneficiary makes no withdrawals and lets the assets grow tax deferred until his or her own death and then passes the money directly to a beneficiary.

CONTRACT DESIGNATIONS

A primary benefit for the variable annuity investor is the right to decide its ownership, beneficiary, and distribution method. The designations of owner, beneficiary, and annuitant are made at the time of purchase. They can be changed at the owner's option. These are important decisions and should be considered carefully.

There are many contract designation combinations and options available to investors. The examples in Tables 10.2 and 10.3 apply to nonqualified annuity contracts: the first illustration is the most common choice. The second option shows the impact to the

TABLE 10.2

Example 1

Intent:	Ownership by husband (wife)
	Husband to receive annuity payments
	Wife receives ownership at husband's death
	Children receive control after both parents' deaths
Owner Designation:	Husband
Annuitant	Husband
Contingent Annuitant:	Wife
Beneficiary	Wife
Contingent Beneficiary:	Children

TABLE 10.3

Example 2

Intent:	Husband and wife are joint owners
	Husband to receive annuity payments
	Children are beneficiaries
Ownership Designation:	Joint
Annuitant	Husband
Beneficiary:	Children

wife of one change. The examples assume that the owner(s) die before the date of annuitization (income date).

In the first example, a husband (who is both the owner and the annuitant) dies. His wife, who is the beneficiary, may continue the contract or annuitize over her life expectancy. In this case, she decides to continue the contract and names her children as beneficiaries. At the wife's death, the children may elect to continue the contract for five years or annuitize the contract within one year.

In the second example, the husband is the owner and the annuitant and the children are the beneficiaries. When the husband dies, the wife is skipped. This can be disastrous if not structured properly. The wife was not listed as a contingent owner or beneficiary and is therefore omitted as having any rights to the funds.

GUARANTEED DEATH BENEFITS

Insurance companies frequently stress the value of the guaranteed death benefit offered by their variable annuity contracts. Contracts guarantee that upon the death of the annuity owner, the beneficiary receives either the value of the contract or 100 percent of the contributions, whichever is greater. An additional benefit of many contracts is a step-up feature in which the contract death benefit is increased after a certain number of years to reflect the most current value of the contract. I will now explain the most common enhanced death benefit options for contract holders, which are: return of premium, annual step, percentage step, and step up every number of years (e.g., 5).

Return of Premium   This option guarantees the beneficiaries that when the annuitant dies, they will receive no less than the original contribution, less previous withdrawal. This is the most basic death benefit option and is also the least expensive.

Annual Step   This option guarantees that the beneficiaries will receive the greatest value of any particular year. For example, let's look at a hypothetical account balance in Table 10.4. If the annuitant

TABLE 10.4

Hypothetical Annuity Value

Year	Account Value on Policy Anniversary
1997	$100,000
1998	$125,000
1999	$150,000
2000	$145,000
2001	$147,500

died in 2001, his heirs would anticipate receiving the balance of $147,500. In actuality, they would receive $150,000 since that was the highest annual step up. The cost for this benefit is much higher than the standard death benefit, since the cost to insure the risk by the insurance company is also higher.

Percentage Step   This option guarantees the beneficiaries will receive the contributions plus an annual interest factor. For example, if an annuitant contributed $100,000 and the contract had a 3 percent annual percentage step up, his heirs would be guaranteed to receive no less than $103,000, minus withdrawals, if the annuitant died in the second year.

Step Up Every Number of Years (e.g., Five)   This option guarantees that the benefit to the heirs will ratchet up if, on the anniversary date in the year the annuitant dies, he was eligible for a step up. For example, if the annuitant chose a five-year step up and, on the fifth policy anniversary, his account value had grown from $100,000 to $150,000, his heirs would not receive less than the $150,000 even if the account plummeted to $50,000 and never improved.

As you can see, the death benefit options are numerous. I hope I have proven in this chapter that the fact that the heirs do not receive a step up at death for taxation is not that big a deal for most investors. I also hope that you better understand how the death benefit options available within the annuity wrapper are a means of further protecting your heirs.

PART TWO

Investment Strategy, Planning, and Common Mistakes

CHAPTER 11

Investment Basics: Understanding Stocks and Bonds

We have outlined the annuity versus mutual fund comparisons; now we need to look at the investment strategy. In order to comprehend the investment strategy section of this book, you first must understand the basics.

UNDERSTANDING STOCKS

A stock is a right of ownership in a corporation. The ownership is divided into a certain number of shares; the corporation issues each stockholder one or more stock certificates that indicate how many shares the stockholder holds. The stockholders own the company and elect a board of directors to manage it for them.

The capital a company raises through the sale of these shares entitles the holder to dividends and to other rights of ownership, such as voting rights.

Prices of stocks change according to general business conditions and the earnings and future prospects of the companies that have issued the stock. If the business is doing well, stockholders may be able to sell their stock for a profit. If it is not, they may have to take a loss.

Large corporations may have many thousands of stockholders. Their stock is bought and sold in marketplaces called stock exchanges. When a sale is made, the buyer owns the seller's shares.

The shares of stock represent the value of the corporation. When the corporation has made a profit, the directors may divide the profit among stockholders as dividends, or they may decide to use it to expand the business. Dividends are paid to the stock shareholders out of the corporation's profits. When profits are used to expand the business, the directors and stockholders may issue more stock to show that there is more money invested in the business. This new stock will be divided among the old stockholders as stock dividends.

WHAT ARE THE MOST COMMON FORMS OF STOCK?

Common Stock

Common stock represents true ownership shares in a company. Stockholders share directly in growing company profits through increasing dividends and an appreciation in the value of the stock itself. As the holder of common stock, you are a part-owner of the company issuing the stock. The purchaser of common stock not only receives a share of any dividends paid by the corporation but also gets the right to vote for corporate directors who, in turn, choose the corporate officers and set the corporation's policies. When your bank investment representative uses the term *stock,* he or she is normally referring to *common* stock. The bulk of investments in most mutual funds will be common stock

Preferred Stock

Preferred stock, like common stock, represents ownership or equity and not debt. Preferred stockholders have a claim on profits which precedes, or has preference over, the claim of the common stockholder. The preferred stockholder has a right to receive *specified* dividends (for example, 10 percent of the face value of the preferred share) before the common stockholder can be paid any dividend at all.

On the other hand, the preferred stockholder does not have the possibility of large gains open to the common stockholder. While the common stockholder may hope for rising dividends if the corporation prospers, the preferred shareholder will receive at most the specified dividend. If the preferred stockholders share with the common stockholders in dividends beyond the specified percentage, the stock is called *participating preferred*.

Preferred stock may also be cumulative. That is, if there are no dividends given in a year, the preferred stockholders must be given double their dividend the next year. This is paid before anything is paid to the common stockholders. This principle continues for as many years as dividends are not paid.

PRICE/EARNINGS RATIO

The price/earnings (P/E) ratio measures the stock's price divided by the company's earnings per share (or EPS) over the past 12 months. If a stock is trading at $25 and earned $1.25 per share over the past four quarters, its P/E ratio is 20 ($25 ÷ $1.25). Value investors look for stocks trading at low P/Es, while growth investors don't mind paying high P/Es if they think the company's profits will be increasing rapidly. Average P/E ratios are also calculated for individual mutual funds. These tell you how the overall portfolio is valued. A growth fund would likely have a higher average P/E than an income-oriented portfolio.

DIVIDEND PAYOUT RATIO

The dividend payout ratio is the ratio of a company's indicated annual cash dividend per share to its earnings per share (EPS), and can range from zero to 100 percent. A utility that pays out $4 in dividends for each $5 of earnings would have a payout of 80 percent. The payout for the average large industrial company is above 50 percent and even higher for the typical utility. The higher the dividend payout, however, the less room there is for dividend increases, since less profit is available to reinvest for future growth.

DIVIDEND YIELD

Dividend yield represents the annual dividend paid on a share of stock divided by the share price. For example, if a utility's dividend is $4 and its stock sells for $50 a share, the yield would be 8 percent. When the EPS (in general) is high, yields will be low.

CLASSIFICATION OF STOCKS

Stocks can be lumped into several broad categories. These are general classifications, and a stock might simultaneously fit into two or more categories. For example, a "blue chip" may also be classified as "growth and income" and "growth." A "value" company may be categorized as "speculative."

> *Growth Stocks:* Common stock of nationally known, high-quality companies. Typically, the companies are large, old, and well established, such as those represented in the Dow Jones Industrial Average.
>
> Growth stocks are often considered income stocks by virtue of their fairly high dividend payouts. Many of the companies included in the S&P 500 would also qualify as growth stocks.
>
> *Value Stocks:* These stocks have a high book-to-market ratio. This means that they are considered a "good buy" since the market is pricing the stock lower than its actual value.

WHY DO STOCKS GO UP AND DOWN?

All stocks fluctuate (change) in value. Circumstances may have lessened the earning power of a company and thus lowered the price that people are willing to pay for shares. Prosperous times or better management may increase values.

HOW PRICES MOVE

The stock market is an open auction, where prices are determined by open outcry on the exchange floor. In order to maintain an orderly, supply-demand auction, "specialists" are designated by the exchanges to handle individual equities. These individuals control stock prices by matching buy and sell orders delivered by the floor brokers shouting out their orders. The specialists change the prices to match the supply and demand fundamentals so loudly surrounding them. The specialist system was created to guarantee that every seller finds a buyer, and vice versa. This process may sound chaotic, but specialists do succeed in their function of maintaining an orderly market and matching sellers to buyers.

TRADING

A person who wishes to buy stock places an order with his or her representative. The representative gets a quotation (price) by telephone and relays the order to the floor of the exchange. The partner negotiates the sale and notifies the brokerage house. The entire transaction may take only a few minutes.

Each year, investors trade billions of shares worth trillions of dollars. Stock prices often reflect the state of the economy: If business conditions are good, stock prices tend to rise, creating a bull market. If conditions are poor, stock prices drop, causing a bear market.

WHERE IS THE STOCK TRADED?

The stock exchange is a marketplace where member brokers (agents) buy and sell stocks and bonds of American and foreign businesses on behalf of the public. A stock exchange provides a marketplace for stocks and bonds in the same way a commodity exchange does for commodities.

To most investors, "the stock market" means the New York Stock Exchange (NYSE), which has been in existence for over 200 years. Needless to say, it has come a long way since 24 merchants and auctioneers met at the site of the present exchange to negotiate an agreement to buy and sell stocks and bonds issued by the new United States government, along with those of a few banks and insurance companies. It wasn't until 1817 that the exchange adopted an approved constitution, whereby it named itself the New York Stock and Exchange Board. The exchange did not cross the million-share daily threshold until 1886. Its dullest day ever was March 16, 1830, when only 31 shares changed hands. In 1997, the exchange witnessed the first day where 1 billion shares were traded.

There are also many other North American exchanges trading stock, from the American Stock Exchange (called AMEX) on down to the Spokane Stock Exchange.

In addition, thousands of equities are not traded on any exchange but are, rather, sold over the counter (OTC). Prices for OTC stocks are readily available through the NASDAQ, an acronym for the National Association of Securities Dealers Automated Quotations system, the hottest market today.

There is a distinct difference between OTC stocks and exchange-listed equities, revolving primarily around eligibility requirements. Each stock exchange has listing requirements that must be met before a company may take its place on the exchange floor. For example, before a stock can be listed on the NYSE, the company must have at least 1 million shares outstanding (available to the public). Those shares must be held by at least 2000 different stockholders, each of whom owns at least 100 shares. The company must also have earned a pretax profit of at least $2.5 million the year preceding the listing, and the pretax profits in the two prior years must have been at least $2 million each year. The AMEX and the regional exchanges have similar (though less stringent) listing requirements, but no such limitations exist for OTC listings.

HOW DOES A STOCK EXCHANGE OPERATE?

Federal and state laws regulate the issuance, listing, and trading of most securities. The Securities and Exchange Commission (SEC) administers the federal laws.

Stocks handled by one or more stock exchanges are called listed stocks. A company that wants to have its stock listed for trading on an exchange must first prove to the exchange that it has enough paid-up capital, is a lawful enterprise, and is in good financial condition. Unlisted securities are sold in over-the-counter trading. Most bonds are sold this way. Many unlisted industrial securities are more speculative (involve more risk) than listed ones.

THE STOCK MARKET BAROMETER

When the stock market is said to be up 10 points, what is usually meant is that the venerable Dow Jones Industrial Average (DJIA) went up 10 points. The DJIA is based on the average prices paid for 30 blue-chip stocks. The up-and-down fluctuations of the New York Stock Exchange have been recorded since 1896, and general upward and downward movements of stock prices are symbolized on Wall Street by bulls and bears.

Because the DJIA is weighted through only 30 positions, and because the actual constituents of the average can be (and have been) changed, many market analysts question its validity. The Standard & Poor's 500 Index, the Value Line Composite Index, and the New York Stock Exchange Composite Index are ostensibly more accurate indices and are also more widely followed. These are broader-based, which should make them somewhat more accurate in a large market. Since the DJIA consists of only 30 large companies, it may not truly reflect all aspects of market performance. You should also be familiar with and review other indices such as the Russell 2000 and Wilshire 5000. These each measure different segments of the market based on the size of the stocks. The Wilshire 5000 is the most comprehensive of the indices. The Russell 2000 measures the small caps.

UNDERSTANDING BONDS

What is a *bond?* Don't be ashamed if you don't know. A recent survey by Russ Alan Prince and Karen Maru File indicates that about 88 percent of the affluent are in the dark in this area. In fact, the majority of people who have actually invested in stocks and bonds don't really understand what makes a bond different from all other types of investments. A bond is the legal evidence of a debt, usually the result of a loan of money.

Very important is what backs the bond. In the case of many corporate securities, nothing more is behind them than the full faith and credit of the companies that issue them. These bonds, usually called debentures, are probably the most common type of debt issued by industrial corporations today.

Public utilities generally issue bonds with specific assets as collateral against the loan. These are called mortgage bonds or collateral trust bonds. Some utilities, however, issue debentures, and some industrial corporations issue collateralized bonds.

There are three main categories of bond issuers: (1) the U.S. government or one of its agencies, (2) corporations, and (3) municipalities. While these three types of bonds have some different characteristics, they share a basic structure.

When you buy a bond, you are in effect lending your money to the issuer of the bond. The issuer agrees to make periodic interest payments to you (the investor holding the bond), and also agrees to repay the original sum (the principal) in full to you on a certain date, known as the bond's maturity date. Interest rates can soar and you, the customer, will still be repaid the entire principal at maturity. Interest payments are certain and there will be no volatility with the investment, whereas even a mutual fund with a stable NAV will be affected to some extent by changes in interest rates.

INDIVIDUAL BONDS VERSUS BOND FUNDS

Buying an individual bond gives you much greater control of both cashflow and tax consequences than investing in a bond fund. The owner of an individual bond controls when to take profits and losses based on what is in his or her best interest. If it matters to an investor whether a tax gain is taken in December or January, an individual bond allows that choice.

There is a lot to understand before buying an individual bond. It is a somewhat different process from buying stocks or mutual funds, because only a certain dollar amount of each bond is issued and that amount is almost certainly much smaller than the amount of equity issued. Large companies have millions of shares of stock outstanding, and all shares of common stock are the same. To buy a bond, on the other hand, the customer can't simply consult *The Wall Street Journal*, pick a particular bond, and place an order. Buying a bond means finding the owner (such as an institutional trading desk) of a bond that meets your needs.

Following is information an investor should consider before making an individual bond purchase:

- Security description: type of bond, purpose of the bond, and issuer
- Rating: for example, A or AA
- Trade date: the date the bond is purchased in the market
- Settlement date: the date the purchaser pays for the bond and interest starts accruing
- Maturity date: the date the purchaser will be repaid the principal and last interest payment.
- Interest payment dates: the dates interest payments are made, usually semiannually

- Coupon: fixed annual interest rate (interest income) stated on the bond
- Price: dollar price paid for the bond (An *offer* price is the price at which the individual investor buys the bond; the *bid* price is the price at which the individual can sell the bond.)
- Current yield: the coupon divided by price, giving a rough approximation of cashflow
- Yield to maturity: measure of total return on the bond
- Par amount: face amount of the bond
- Accrued interest: the amount of interest income (coupon income) earned from the date of the last coupon payment to settlement date; all bonds trade at value plus accrued interest.
- Interest calculation: whether the bond uses a 360-day or 365-day basis to calculate interest payments
- Special features: features specific to a bond that can affect value, trading characteristics, and so on.

The main form of market risk for a bond is interest-rate risk, that is the risk of interest rates changing after a customer buys the bond. If market interest rates go up, the bond loses principal value; if market rates go down, the bond gains principal value. The longer the term of the bond, the more the price will be affected by changes in interest rates. Whether the U.S. government, a corporation, or a municipality issues the bond, the risk is similar.

Bonds are also subject to call risk, the risk that the bond issuer will choose to redeem (call) the bond before the maturity date. The call provisions must be stated in the prospectus along with other special features, but a prospectus can be hard to understand.

A LOOK AT INTEREST RATES

A bond's current value is directly affected by changes in the interest rates. The effect of higher interest rates on bonds is to lower their prices. Conversely, lower rates raise bond prices. The fluctuation is due to the fact that the price of the bond must offer a prospective purchaser current market rates. For instance, a previously issued bond with a 12 percent coupon is worth almost 20 percent over par (face value) when newly issued bonds are only paying 10 percent; and a bond with an 8 percent coupon will sell for about 80 percent of par if current rates move to 10 percent.

RATING SERVICES

The two major independent rating services, Moody's and Standard & Poor's, conduct thorough financial investigations of bond issues on an ongoing basis. Investment-grade ratings range from AAA to BBB (Standard & Poor's), or Aaa to Baa3 (Moody's) (see Table 11.1). Lower-rated bonds are considered speculative. Many advisors will confine their attention to bonds rated A or above.

Ratings attempt to assess the probability that the issuing company will make timely payments of interest and principal. Each rating service has slightly different evaluation methods. Ratings are intended to help you evaluate risk and set your own standards for investment.

Strong credit backing does not eliminate market risk. The price of any bond fluctuates in harmony with the rise and fall of interest rates in general and the stability of the underlying corporation or agency issuing the bond.

TYPES OF BONDS

Corporate Bonds

Corporations of every size and credit quality issue corporate bonds, from the very best blue-chip companies to small companies with low ratings. The first thing to find out about a bond is its credit rating, which is supplied by large rating agencies.

Corporate bonds are not easy to evaluate, especially those with longer maturities when call provisions may apply and the credit outlook is less certain. Many investors simply choose to stay in shorter maturities, or with extremely sound companies such as utilities. Corporate bonds may be backed by collateral and are fully taxable at the federal, state, and local levels.

Yields are higher on corporate bonds than on a CD or government-insured bonds. The coupon is fixed and return

TABLE 11.1

Bond Ratings

Claims Paying Ability	Standard & Poors
Superior	AAA
Excellent	AA
Good	A
Adequate	BBB
May Be Adequate	BB
Vulnerable	B
Extremely Vulnerable	CCC
Regulatory Action	R

Claims Paying Ability	Duff & Phelps
Highest	AAA
Very High	AA–, AA, AA+
High	A–, A, A+
Adequate	BBB–, BBB, BBB+
Uncertain	BB–, BB, BB+
Possessing Risk	B–, B, B+
Substantial Risk	CCC
Liquidation	DD

Claims Paying Ability	Moody's
Exceptional	Aaa
Excellent	Aa
Good	A
Adequate	Baa
Questionable	Ba
Poor	B
Very Poor	Caa
Extremely Poor	Ca
Lowest	C

Claims Paying Ability	A.M. Best
Superior	A+, A++
Excellent	A–, A
Very Good	B+, B++
Fair	B–, B
Marginal	C+, C++
Weak	C–, C
Poor	D
Under Regulatory Supervision	E
In Liquidation	F
Rating Suspended	S

of principal is guaranteed by the issuer if the investor holds it until maturity. If the investor sells the bond prior to maturity, the bond will be subject to market fluctuation. Investors who want to be able to check the prices of their bonds in the newspaper should buy listed bonds, preferably those listed on the New York Stock Exchange.

The fully taxable nature of corporate bonds (as opposed to municipals or U.S. Treasuries) has an effect on yield. When buying an AAA-rated corporate bond, you are buying a security that has more risk than a U.S. government bond. For the risk you are taking, you should receive an additional 25 to 50 basis points in yield.

U.S. GOVERNMENT NOTES AND BONDS

The U.S. government issues both Treasury notes (with maturities of 2 to 10 years) and bonds (maturities over 10 years). The government auctions U.S. government securities on a regular quarterly schedule. U.S. government securities are considered to have no credit risk, and their rate of return is the benchmark by which all other market rates of return are measured.

TREASURY BILLS

Treasury bills (T-bills) are a U.S. financial security issued by the Federal Reserve bank for the Treasury as a means of borrowing money for short periods of time. They are sold at a discount from their maturity value, pay no coupons, and have maturities of 30 days to 1 year. Because they are a direct obligation of the federal government, they are free of default risk. Most Treasury bills are purchased by commercial banks and held as a part of their secondary reserves.

In a normal yield-curve environment, U.S. government notes typically have yields 50 to 250 basis points higher than those on T-bills and 50 to 250 basis points lower than U.S. government bonds. Notes are the most likely investment for an individual investor because of the maturity range. Institutional investors and traders actively trade the 30-year bond.

MUNICIPAL BONDS

What are municipal bonds? Very simply, they are investment instruments used to finance municipal governmental activities. They are not always guaranteed by the municipality.

Investors whose goal is simply to conserve capital and generate returns that keep up with inflation often look to municipal bonds with the idea that these bonds are fairly safe. Investors may believe this because municipal issuances often have language stating that they are "backed by the full faith and credit of the issuing authority." The combination of apparent safety and tax-free income seems irresistible to many who are not especially sophisticated about the securities markets and who are seeking simply to avoid making an investment mistake.

Munis attract many wealthy investors for the reasons just stated. Unfortunately, a detailed analysis of the total return on tax-free municipal bonds does not always justify the exemption from tax. If your total tax-free return is 5 percent and you are in the 40 percent tax bracket, you are looking at a taxable return of approximately 8.3 percent. If you can do better than 8.3 percent in a taxable account or in a variable annuity, you may be better off investing outside municipal bonds.

There are other reasons a muni investment is not a very good one. If rates fall and prices rise, you are not necessarily going to be able to take advantage of your good fortune because the municipalities have the right to call the bonds, thereby returning your investment early. You should also remember that tax-free does not mean risk-free; the Orange County debacle of the early 1990s is an example of the potential downside of not being properly diversified.

Finally, municipal bonds may also have high trading costs. This is because there are sometimes large bid/ask spreads and significant market impact costs in the municipal marketplace. These additional costs can eliminate the benefit of using an active trading strategy. The turnover required would be simply too costly. I would only recommend individual muni bonds for those with long time horizons and too risk averse to be in the equity markets.

BOND FUNDS

An investor with less than $50,000 to invest in bonds is probably better off in a bond fund (called a Unit Investment Trust). A bond fund is nothing more than a portfolio of bonds. Most bond funds invest in bonds of similar maturity (the number of years before the borrower must pay back the money to the lender). For example, a short-term bond fund concentrates its investments in bonds maturing in less than 5 years. Intermediate funds generally hold bonds that come due within 5 to 15 years. Long-term funds usually require investment for 15 years or more. The key advantage of a bond fund is management. Unlike individual issues, the fund managers can switch bonds from time to time within a fund. A bond fund is always replacing bonds in its portfolio to maintain its average maturity objective.

Bond funds provide the advantages of diversification, professional management, and significant cost benefits. An institutional investor buys bonds more cheaply than a single individual, and the bonds in a mutual fund have been purchased at the institutional price. The institutional investor also pays a minuscule portion of total price in transaction costs, whereas transaction costs can be significant for an individual, and it gets worse if the individual must pay for safekeeping the securities. A bond fund does, however, charge a management fee that might equal in yield the transaction cost an individual would pay, but the diversification offered by the bond fund makes up for this. The bond fund pays dividends monthly since it owns bonds with so many different payment dates, whereas individual bonds pay out only semiannually.

MUNICIPAL BOND FUNDS

Municipal bond funds are nothing more than a large grouping of various municipal bonds. They may be appropriate when you are in a high federal tax bracket (greater than 28 percent) and if you are using state-specific muni bond funds in a high state tax bracket (greater than 5 percent). Most municipal bond funds invest in municipal bonds of similar maturity (the number of years before the borrower, in this case the municipality, must pay back the money to you, the lender).

Single-state funds buy bonds issued in just one state and pay interest that is usually free of state and federal taxes. Interest from national municipal bond funds, which own bonds from several states, is free from federal, but generally not state, taxes.

To determine if a muni fund makes sense for you, compare your after-tax return to another type of bond or equity fund. A simple way of doing this is by dividing your tax-free return by (100 – your tax rate).

1997 was a tough year for almost all muni bond funds. 1998 is off to a similar start. The reason is that interest rate fears have been sending the bond market on a roller-coaster ride as the equity markets continue to roll along at a higher than expected growth pattern.

In summation, there are several different types of stocks and bonds. The typical consumer is unable to investigate all of the options. I therefore strongly recommend a selection of mutual funds and variable annuity sub-accounts that leave the research up to the professionals.

Next, let's review an investment strategy that utilizes the fundamentals we just discussed.

CHAPTER 12

Why an Investment Strategy?

Okay, you've learned the value of the variable annuity by reading Part One, and the last chapter helped you understand the basics. But how do you get started on investing? You need to decide how much to invest and in what. Do you need growth or do you want to protect what you already have? If you need growth, you need to invest in equities (stocks).

But there's a problem. You can't have absolute assurance and growth too. Annuity customers are generally very comfortable with fixed-interest annuity investments because they do not fluctuate in value, but not everyone is comfortable with equities. The trick is achieving growth within the comfort zone of an annuity. To achieve growth or higher rates of return with an annuity, you need an investment strategy.

The following chapters present methods of investing that provide a strategy for the variable annuity customer, combining both fixed and growth investments to reach those higher yields we all are seeking.

Let's start by examining why you need a strategy. Inflation is historically running at about 3 percent a year at this writing. Someone who only holds savings deposits with no interest is losing purchasing power. This is extremely important when you consider that the investments you make today may be your only source of income tomorrow. It is critical to maximize your savings dollars investment returns. To stay even with a 4 percent annual inflation rate, your investments must increase by at least that amount every year. Unfortunately, most bank CDs today are only paying 5 percent before tax, which is equal to only 3.5 percent if you pay 30 percent in taxes. This is just barely keeping pace with inflation. Many investors who originally purchased CDs at higher rates have since had to reinvest at lower rates. This comes as a shock when planning has been largely dependent on higher original interest rates. The answer is to do it differently.

INVEST IN EQUITIES

Equities means stocks or mutual funds. A well-managed stock portfolio can provide a dependable long-term inflation hedge. Clearly, common stocks have produced and should continue to produce returns that will outpace the thief of inflation. You may have seen a chart similar to Figure 12.1

Notice the gap between common stocks and T-Bonds. It's the gap that we all want and need to fill. That's why a component of common stocks (mutual funds/sub-accounts) in a variable annuity portfolio is so important.

A PROVEN METHOD OF INVESTING

A time-proven way to get started if you are averse to risk is to use dollar cost averaging. People coming into a variable annuity from a fixed-interest account will commonly utilize this annuity option. It is simply the investing of equal dollar amounts at regular intervals—monthly, quarterly, or annually. It's an effective method that can help you turn the characteristic fluctuation of common stock value into a benefit. When prices are low, you will be able to purchase more shares. When prices are higher, you will purchase fewer shares. Over time, you will purchase a greater number of shares at lower price levels, making your average cost per share generally lower than the average of the price at which shares are purchased (see Figure 12.2). For this strategy to be effective, you should consider your ability to continue investing equal amounts at regular intervals, even through periods of low price levels. The

FIGURE 12.1

Asset Allocation: 25-Year Annualized Returns and Growth of
a Dollar (1971–1995)

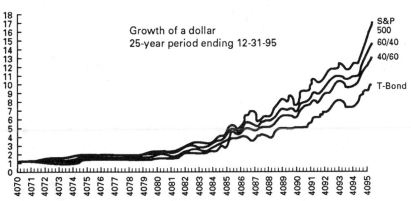

Asset allocation: 25-year annualized returns and growth (from Larry Chambers,
The Prudent Investor's Guide).

objective of dollar cost averaging is to purchase shares at an average cost below the average price.

The example in Figure 12.2 charts a $150-per-month investment through a 10-month period. Share price has fluctuated during this time, but the investment amount is held constant. When prices are low ($2), you will be able to purchase more shares (75). When prices are higher ($10), you will purchase fewer shares (15). In total you will purchase 342.5 shares, and you will purchase a greater number of those shares at lower price levels, thereby making your average cost per share ($4.38) lower than the average price ($6) at which shares are purchased.

It is easy to look at the options and decide to invest 100 percent in U.S. blue chip-stocks. It is also easy to say that dollar cost averaging is the answer to your dreams of lowering your average share price, thus increasing returns. The problem is that these actions individually do not compose a strategy. A strategy is the combination of several components—such as diversification, asset allocation, proper time consideration, structuring assets to allow for proper liquidity, and a commitment to stay on track with your investments in good years and bad.

FIGURE 12.2

Dollar Cost Averaging

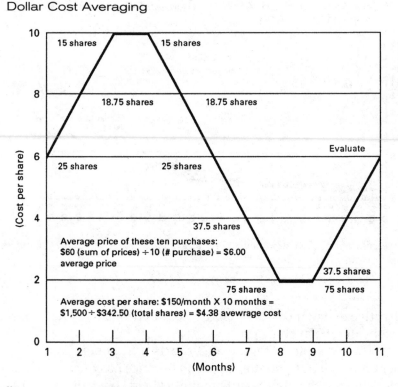

Dollar cost averaging. The objective is to purchase shares at an average cost below the average price (from Larry Chambers, *First Time Investor*).

In the next chapter, I will provide information that has been written and rewritten hundreds of times. Some of the principles are basic, while others can be very confusing. Take your time and understand the building blocks.

CHAPTER 13

Components of an Investment Strategy

Now that you understand *why*, let's look at *how*. Let's say that you agree you need equities in your variable annuity portfolio, now what? Next, you need a strategy for implementation of an equity or mutual fund component within your portfolio.

INVESTMENT PRINCIPLES

There are certain principles for investing that have withstood the test of time and that have served to reduce risk, no matter what type of investments were made. One of the best strategies is to create the right balance among various investments in a broadly diversified portfolio. This was expertly reported in what is generally known as Modern Portfolio Theory by Professors Harry Markowitz and William Sharpe, winners of the 1990 Nobel Prize in Economic Science. Now taught in virtually every graduate business school in the country, Modern Portfolio Theory instructs investors on just how to achieve higher returns while minimizing risk by diversifying investments into different asset classes and following the principles of asset allocation.

In the 16-year bull run that began in August 1982, the S&P 500 outpaced the mutual funds aggressive growth fund index 1334 percent to 931 percent, notwithstanding the latter's admittedly greater risk-taking style. But during different periods of time, the reverse was true. For example, since the Persian Gulf crisis ended in 1990, aggressive growth of 23 percent eclipsed the S&P 500's 20 percent, based on average returns. We will explain the differences between total return and average return later, but you can see how they can be confusing. Simply, one is the total that would represent the growth of a dollar while the other adds annual returns and divides by the number of years.

The *total return* is the most complete measure of performance. Total return considers the price increase or decrease of an asset, along with its income or yield generated after taxes and other fees. For example, in measuring the total annual return of a bond fund, the income earned from the bond is added to the changes in the price of the bond before the resulting sum is divided by the value of the bond at the beginning of the time period measured.

Capital appreciation return is defined as the total return minus any income or dividends of the security.

Average return is the measure of price of an asset, along with its income or yield on average over a specific time period. The *compound return* is different than the average return in that the compound includes the growth of interest on the interest. In other words, like an annuity, the compound return takes into consideration the value of time as a means of accumulating interest on accumulated interest.

Expected return is calculated as the weighted average of its possible returns where the weights are the corresponding probability for each return.

THE FIRST COMPONENT IS DIVERSIFICATION

Diversification means not having all your money in any one type of investment. Mutual funds, by design, are diversified. Investing in mutual funds is the first step you can take in reducing investment risk. Your overall investment performance should be less volatile if you are in a broad variety of investments rather than in a single type. The graphs in Figure 13.1 illustrate the importance of diversification.

Graph 1 illustrates a single investment of $10,000 at an 8 percent return over 25 years. Graph 2 illustrates diversifying the same

FIGURE 13.1

The Power of Diversification as an Investment Strategy

Graph 1   Graph 2

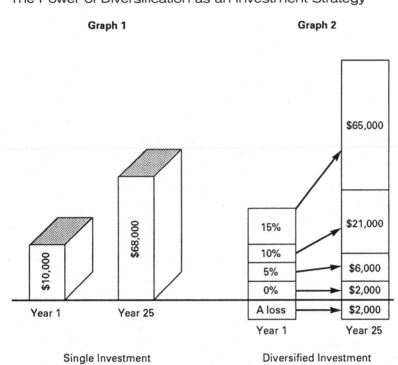

Single Investment   Diversified Investment

The power of diversification as an investment strategy (from Larry Chambers, *Wrap Free*).

$10,000 investment into five separate $2000 investments representing various returns. While three of the five investments showed a lower return than the single investment, the total for the diversified side was substantially higher. While it's true you would have been further ahead with all your money invested in the "hot" fund, that's just luck, and you're unlikely to predict beforehand which is going to be the next "hot" fund.

Each asset responds differently to changes in the economy or the investment marketplace. As we discussed earlier, when interest rates drop, stocks take off. If you look back at the 1970s and 1980s, the market was down while interest rates and real estate soared. The trick is to own a variety of assets, because a short-term decline in one can be balanced by others that are stable or going up in value.

The stock market may go up one year and down the next, while other investments such as CDs might remain unchanged. In this case, investors who own both shares of a stock fund as well as bond funds will be better off than those who limit themselves to stocks only.

The higher volatility of stocks and bonds means higher risk. Suppose all your money was invested in stocks and you needed to sell some of your holdings to meet an emergency. If the stocks in your mutual funds were depressed when you needed to sell, you could be forced to take a loss on your investment. Forget the tax deferral for now, that's only part of the equation. Owning other investments would give you flexibility in raising needed cash while allowing you to hold your stocks until those prices improved.

The Good News Is . . .

During the long run, owning a wide variety of investments has been the best strategy. Money market funds or cash can provide a foundation of stability and liquidity that is ideal for cash reserve. Bonds are good for steady high income, and stocks have the greatest potential for superior long-term returns. Diversification can reduce, but not totally eliminate, risk and is the most prudent method for managing investment risk.

Not All Diversification Is Effective

If all investments owned were diverse but likely to decrease in value at the same time, that type of diversification would be ineffective. This was the premise of Harry Markowitz's Nobel Prize-winning theory. He showed that, to the extent that securities in a portfolio do not move in concert with each other, their individual risks could be effectively diversified away. Effective diversification reduces portfolio price changes in mutual funds and smooths out return when coupled with investments such as bank CDs and fixed-income investments.

Simple Strategy 1: Buy One Asset Class

Investing in an asset class that contains many securities of different companies will help you to avoid the risks that are present if you invest in securities of only a few companies or companies in only one industry. The economy and the financial markets are ever changing. Spreading your investment among many different companies in different industries can significantly reduce the risk of unpleasant surprises. Sub-accounts (mutual funds) are designed to give you this type of effective diversity.

Simple Strategy 2: Invest in Different Asset Classes

The other type of diversification is to spread your investments among different types of asset classes such as bond funds and stock funds. Each of these securities has different risks and will fluctuate in value over time. Selecting different types of investments will help reduce the risks present when owning only one type of security.

By combining equity-based asset classes with the stability of predictable returns (short-term fixed investments), studies show, your overall portfolio will have the best opportunity for growth. This combined strategy reduces price fluctuations in your overall portfolio and increases compounded returns.

So, there are two types of diversification: diversification among different companies within a single asset class, and diversification among different types of asset classes. Both are necessary.

THE SECOND COMPONENT IS ASSET ALLOCATION

The simple strategy of 60/40—60 percent in the equity market and 40 percent in the bond market—is the basis of asset allocation. Pension plans have used this strategy for the last 30 years.

Research has shown that the asset allocation decision—how you split your investments up among various asset categories such as equities and bonds—has by far the greatest impact on your overall investment performance. Diversification is spreading the wealth; asset allocation is structuring your diversification.

As illustrated in Figure 13.2, more than 90 percent of total return variation is due to the asset allocation of your portfolio. In contrast, stock market timing and stock selection account for less than 7 percent. You are not going to hear much about this from your stockbroker, no matter how friendly he is, not even if your stock-

FIGURE 13.2

Determinants of Portfolio Return

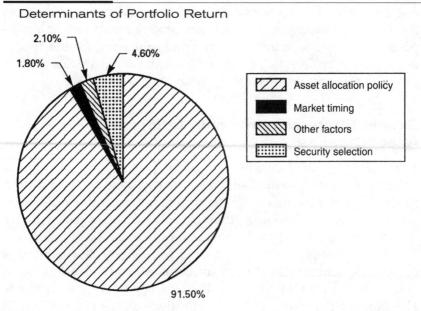

broker is your brother-in-law. No one wants to tell you that the service he or she is providing will only amount to 7 percent of your overall investment performance. Determining the right asset allocation can be critical to your investment success. Although often used interchangeably, don't confuse asset allocation with diversification. They are not the same thing.

Asset allocation is a means of matching asset classes that perform differently to reduce the overall risk in a portfolio. During certain time periods, some asset classes will be up and some will be down; you want a mix of these types. The overall mathematical result of asset allocation is that you reduce risk to a greater degree than by simply diversifying.

Allocating assets in appropriate amounts among asset classes results in diversification that limits risk and enhances or stabilizes rates of return inside the variable annuity. The idea is to get the maximum possible return for a given level of risk. Tools for asset allocation range from a pen and notepad to sophisticated software programs. Software-assisted asset allocation is becoming common in many investment programs. The use of software takes the guess-work out of the process. This is where an investment advisor or financial planner can really earn his fees.

"Noise investors" believe that by regularly reading *The Wall Street Journal* or some other financial publication, they become in-siders to information that gives them some advantage. But like most mutual funds, most noise investors significantly underperform the market. Noise investors are those who listen to and act on the buzz on the street or in the papers.

What noise investors don't realize is that some mutual fund managers focus on market timing, which is costly to implement, has an extremely low probability of success, and is ineffective in adding value. As previously mentioned, this management strategy contributes less than 7 percent of a portfolio's profit determination. Academic studies have found that, as I've shown earlier, over 90 percent of returns are generated from making the right asset allo-cation decisions.

"Information investors" do just the opposite of noise investors. Information investors take the time to understand how financial markets actually work and use this financial market knowledge to make money consistently.

An information investor will focus on the overall investment strategy and portfolio, rather than viewing a specific investment in isolation. Academic studies tell us that each investment should be evaluated as to its contribution to a portfolio's *total* return. Risk is not best viewed on an asset-by-asset basis, which is the common practice of noise investors.

Tables 13.1 through 13.6 show the strategy of an information investor, presented in a six-step, easy-to-follow, building-block ap-proach. Each step of the process is designed to maintain an equal level of risk. By applying this strategy, you can significantly in-crease your ending wealth. These steps are the culmination of over 50 years of academic research. By not getting caught up in the noise and not trying to second-guess the direction of the market by picking hot stocks or mutual funds, you can focus on utilizing academic research to increase the likelihood of achieving your long-term financial goals. Most of the advisors I work with follow a strategy like this one. What you will see is how a portfolio that begins with a simple 60/40 equity-to-bond split can be adjusted

TABLE 13.1

Step One

Portfolios	Years	Geometric Mean %	Standard Deviation	Growth of $1
60% Equity – 40% Bond Mutual Funds	19	12.02	10.89	8.65

TABLE 13.2

Step Two

Portfolios	Years	Geometric Mean %	Standard Deviation	Growth of $1
60% S&P 500 – 40% S/L Intermed. Bonds	19	12.10	10.93	8.77

for different asset classes, thus increasing returns and lowering volatility. (Notice that in each of the following six steps standard deviation remains about the same and the growth of the dollar increases.)

The most often recommended portfolio allocation from investment professionals has been 60 percent in the equity market and 40 percent in the bond market; that's shown in Step One (Table 13.1). Most financial advisors use this single strategy.

If you had done nothing more than use the most basic of asset class mutual funds from the Standard & Poor's 500 and the Shearson Lehman International Bond (as shown in Step Two, Table 13.2), you would have accomplished approximately the same return at the same level of risk.

Substituting short-term fixed-income for long-term fixed-income (Step Three, Table 13.3) significantly reduces risk while increasing expected returns. This reduction in risk (standard deviation) will allow you to introduce other riskier asset classes, such as international equity.

TABLE 13.3

Step Three

Portfolios	Years	Geometric Mean %	Standard Deviation	Growth of $1
Shorten Fixed Maturities	19	12.31	10.45	9.08

TABLE 13.4

Step Four

Portfolios	Years	Geometric Mean %	Standard Deviation	Growth of $1
Add Global Diversifi-cation	19	13.06	9.66	10.30

Foreign markets and domestic markets do not move in tandem. With the addition of international investments (Step Four, Table 13.4), you will increase effective diversification. In this example, the 60 percent allocation in equity was divided between the S&P 500 Index and the EAFE (Europe, Australasia, and Far East) Index.

In Step Five (Table 13.5), we have reduced the large equity asset classes by one-third and reallocated that in small asset classes around the world.

Step Six (Table 13.6) involves the book-to-market risk factor. A high book-to-market (high BtM) means that a company's accounting value is high relative to its stock market value. Companies with a high BtM tend to be showing poor earnings or possibly even financial distress. For many investors, it is counterintuitive to buy stock in a company that has poor earnings since we have all been taught to own blue-chip growth companies. However, it is for this very reason that these stocks get a higher return, much like a banker would charge more to a company that does not have good earning prospects. Domestically, this type of stock carries no more risk than

TABLE 13.5

Step Five

Portfolios	Years	Geometric Mean %	Standard Deviation	Growth of $1
Introduce Size Effect	19	14.24	8.68	12.55

TABLE 13.6

Step Six

Portfolios	Years	Geometric Mean %	Standard Deviation	Growth of $1
Utilize The High Btm Risk Factor	19	15.93	9.78	15.93

the market as a whole and even averages 3 percent more per year of growth. I will note that it is difficult in almost all annuities to add this factor.

As you can see by these tables, even if you can only incorporate two or three of the recommended steps, you are historically improving upon the basic 60/40 portfolio.

Each of these six steps will enhance your return while lowering risk by utilizing academic, institutionally tested research. You move from being a noise investor to being an information investor when you start to understand how to implement proven strategies to achieve financial success.

THE THIRD COMPONENT IS TIME

The secret to investment success is time. This one is my favorite because we can all count on time and there is nothing to do but wait.

Given enough time, investments that might otherwise seem unattractive may become highly desirable. The longer the time period over which investments are held, the closer actual returns in a portfolio will come to the expected average. This means short-term market fluctuations will smooth out.

The real challenge is to commit to a discipline of long-term investing and avoid compelling investment distractions. Commit to the strategy. With a long-term view, you can better choose investments that have the best chances for success. By adding the essential ingredient of time to your investment plans, you can almost be assured of success.

Beware of conventional approaches that measure rates of returns over one-year periods. While this is a widely used method, this 12-month time frame simply is not the best measure for all investors with their differing constraints and purposes.

Do not listen to the news media because they also have an extremely short time frame, often that particular day! The media plays to the public's belief that gurus exist who can accurately predict when the market will turn up or down, and that a knowledgeable person can pick the *right* individual security or mutual fund. But every year, about half or more of the mutual funds don't outperform their benchmarks, and those in the upper half in one year have only about a 50 percent chance of repeating in any other year. Look for those sub-accounts that have low turnover, which equals long-term investing.

The media lately have been thrashing international stocks and telling everyone to sell. In 1997, my own international small stock portfolio was down nearly 30 percent. In 1998, it was up about 10 percent in January alone. If I had listened to the media, I would have moved out of international and into U.S. stocks and been even farther behind.

When you look at long-term common stock investments, ups and downs tend to straighten out. Wars and threats of wars become merely blips on the chart. Economic events are put in their proper long-term perspective.

Figure 13.3, showing a "correlation of risk over time," presents another way of looking at how time affects risk. Notice that one-year-at-a-time rates of return on common stocks over the years are almost incoherent, showing both large gains and large losses. Shifting to five-year periods brings a considerable increase in coherence and regularity. The losses are not as great, and the gains appear more consistently. Shifting to 10-year periods increases the consis-

FIGURE 13.3

Various Time Periods, 1950–1980

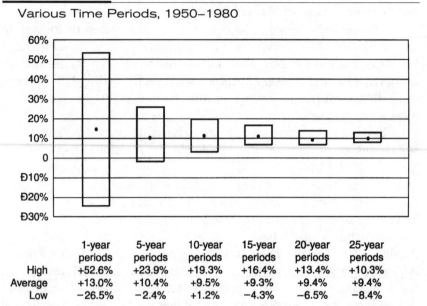

	1-year periods	5-year periods	10-year periods	15-year periods	20-year periods	25-year periods
High	+52.6%	+23.9%	+19.3%	+16.4%	+13.4%	+10.3%
Average	+13.0%	+10.4%	+9.5%	+9.3%	+9.4%	+9.4%
Low	−26.5%	−2.4%	+1.2%	−4.3%	−6.5%	−8.4%

Correlation of risk over time.

tency of returns significantly. Only one loss is experienced, and most periods show positive average annual gains.

Compounding over a decade overwhelms the single-year differences. Looking at 20-year periods brings even more consistency. *There are no losses, only gains.* And the gains cluster more and more closely together around the long-term expected average rate of return.

Even with the obvious substantial differences in the range or distribution of returns in each time frame, there is one central constant: The average actual rate of return is almost the same in all cases. Patterns that seem random or confusing when viewed or experienced day by day, month by month, or year by year take on a splendidly predictable average over time. Analysis shows that, over and over again, the trade-off between risk and reward is driven by one key factor—*time.*

No sensible investor would knowingly invest in a common stock for only one day, month, or even year. Such brief time periods are clearly too short for investment in common stocks, because the expected variation in returns is too large in comparison to the average expected return. Such short-term holdings in common stocks are not investments, they are speculations.

Now, change the measurement period to a longer horizon, and the expected rates of returns and expected variation in returns also change. If we measure an investment every three years, rather than every quarter, we can see satisfying progress that wouldn't be apparent on a quarterly measurement.

In most cases, the time horizon that investors use as the standard to measure results is far too short, causing dissatisfaction with investment performance. (This is perpetuated because stock brokerage firms reward their brokers for the amount of trades or transactions per year, not on how well clients have done.)

Lengthening time horizons requires patience. Uncertainty often causes investors to run out of patience with their investments at the worst possible times—say, at the top of a bull market or the bottom of a bear market. In bull markets, for example, the emotional element often causes investors to increase their holdings in stocks by selling the "underperforming" fixed-income portion of their portfolio, only to become overexposed in expensive stocks at market highs.

These same investors often do just the opposite in bear markets. They liquidate stocks that have declined in value precipitously and buy fixed income securities at market lows. When the stock market recovers, they are no longer positioned to take advantage of the shift.

The ability to maintain patience during difficult times requires more than just an understanding of the stock markets. It also requires an understanding of your own reactions to uncertainty. Only then can you arrive at a working balance between the desire to achieve the highest return and the need to preserve your capital.

REVIEW

Let's briefly review the three factors of intelligent investing: diversification, asset allocation, and time. In addition, let's not forget the importance of professional investment advice to bring these three factors together.

1. Diversification

Mitigate your risk by investing in sub-accounts that have a large pool of holdings. This will minimize the importance of one or two companies on your portfolio.

2. Asset Allocation

Improve your probability of high returns by investing in different asset classes. Purchase individual sub-accounts that globally represent large cap stocks, small cap stocks, and bonds.

3. Time

Choosing a time horizon is as important as the investments you choose. As we have seen, very high returns and very low returns tend to average out over long periods of time. This enables you to recoup any losses you may incur. Over long periods of time, you can also fully realize the benefits of compounding (see Figure 13.4). Compounding isn't a discipline; it is the result of a long-term time horizon.

Once you understand that lengthening your time horizons will increase the probability of success, you are ready to step off the emotional roller coaster that most investors ride.

FIGURE 13.4

Accumulation Comparison

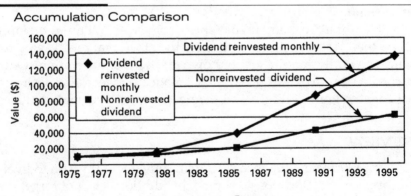

Standard & Poor's 500 index.

4. Professional Advice

Find a reputable investment advisor who understands more than just stocks and bonds. Search out an advisor who understands various types of investments, including annuities. (I'll give you some tips on finding an advisor in Chapter 22.)

Generally speaking, if you smooth out equity returns using proper asset allocation, diversification, and time, over long periods, you can outperform the major indices. Beware, though, that in years like 1997, a 60/40 equity-to-bond globally diversified portfolio accounted for about a 7 percent rate. The S&P 500 however was up almost 30 percent. In years like 1997, it is easy to throw in the towel. Remember, this is long-term. In 1998 and beyond, it is possible that either the international markets or fixed-income investments could outperform the U.S. large cap stocks. Hindsight is 20/20!

CHAPTER 14

Finding Money to Invest in a Variable Annuity

One of the most difficult tasks for investors is being disciplined enough to save. If we all review our income and outlay, most of us will find that there is opportunity to invest. If after reviewing our personal balance sheet, we find we do not have additional disposable dollars, it is time to reduce debt or work harder to live within our means. In this chapter, I will illustrate four simple case studies to show how to do a simple income and expense analysis—and what you should do with the funds you uncover.

IN YOUR THIRTIES: A CASE STUDY

As a member of this age group, I have firsthand knowledge of the issues that face most of us during this decade of life. About half of us are married and of that half perhaps two-thirds have children. I have one child now and plan to have two more. Almost everyone in my subdivision is in a similar situation, with the exception of a few masochists who already have five children. Kids are the focal point of those of us in our thirties who have them, as well as a major economic drain. From an economic perspective, those in their thirties who do not have children should count their economic blessings and stash their cash while they have it. The income range for this segment of the population varies widely.

Let's take a look at a couple's situation, both in their thirties, and first look at what financial actions they have taken so far. Then we will explore together how to implement the recommendations found in this book to increase their net investment return and provide for retirement.

Our couple: Bob and Sue Carter, ages 35 and 34 respectively, have two children, Logan and Kristin (ages 5 and 7). The Carters have a combined income of just under $100,000 and own their home. Their monthly outlay is as follows:

Bills:

Mortgage:	$1,250	(Balance = $150,000 + taxes + insurance)
(2) Cars:	$ 570	(Leased)
Utilities:	$ 300	(Gas, electric, cable, phone, water, garbage)
Food:	$ 300	
Credit Cards:	$ 150	(Balance of $5,000)
Clothing:	$ 100	
Life Insurance:	$ 50	(Term policies on each for $250,000)
Car Insurance:	$ 80	
Miscellaneous:	$ 200	
Total:	**$3,000**	

Savings:

(2) 401(k)s:	$ 750	(500 is 6% of salary; this assumes that their employers match $0.50 on the dollar)
Mutual Funds:	$ 500	
Total	**$1,250**	

Savings Balance:

(2) 401(k)s:	$52,000
Mutual Funds:	$24,000
Total	**$76,000**

At current expected inflation rates of college education, the approximate cost of four-year degrees for two children ages 5 and 7 will be $160,000. This is factored on a current cost of $80,000 at a 7 percent inflation rate. If the Carters continue to save at their current rate in mutual funds, they will have just enough at 10 percent interest compounded to pay 100 percent of the college bill from their mutual fund or 401(k) investment loans. If they were to require 25 percent of the funds to come from their children, the

Carters would be left with about $40,000 to add to and compound. Obviously this is not enough to build on for retirement unless the Carters are able to invest 30 to 40 percent of their income when their kids are out of college.

A better way would be to look at the amount of money that is currently being spent versus earned. The Carters have about $1500 extra each month that could be invested while still maintaining sufficient liquidity outside relatively nonliquid investments. The $1500 represents the difference between net income (after tax) of approximately $5500 a month minus bills and savings.

If they placed $1000 of this into a variable annuity each month, at age 60 they could have over $1.3 million dollars just in the annuity. They would also have additional money and liquidity from $500 a month they place in mutual funds, and their 401(k)s should be worth an additional $1.6 million. The Carters would be looking at a comfortable retirement. This additional $500 a month will enable the Carters to fund a majority of their kids' education without taking loans from their 401(k)s.

The Carters should definitely place that available $1000 in a low-cost variable annuity. Based on their age and savings balance, this is their very best option. As illustrated earlier, they would end up with far less value and income if they chose mutual funds. They have adequately met their liquidity needs through the $500 each month they currently save in mutual funds.

At retirement, the Carters could annuitize their variable annuity. The annuity money could provide them with a net after-tax income of $58,000 at age 60 and grow incrementally to $155,000 by age 80. This income would not be guaranteed as to the amount, but they would be guaranteed income for life. They could use the mutual fund money for liquidity needs in retirement and take systematic withdrawals from their 401(k)s in the amount of approximately $60,000 net after tax. This would give them a combined net income of about $120,000 after tax, which should enable the Carters to live a comfortable lifestyle at that point.

An income today of $100,000 at 3 percent inflation would be equivalent to $212,000 income in 25 years. The Carters would not be making a dramatic leap forward in lifestyle at retirement, but unlike about 97 percent of people today, their lifestyle would not decline.

IN YOUR FORTIES: A CASE STUDY

Statistically, the majority of people who are 40-something are married with two children. The children range in age from very young (3 years) to graduating college. Those who are not married or who are divorced have similar concerns at this age. The top concerns for this group are retirement planning, followed by college education savings. The availability of funds for savings is usually more substantial in the forties group than in the thirties.

If you are 40-something and have not begun your retirement savings plan, you will need a significantly higher savings rate than those who started even a modest plan a decade earlier. I've included a chart (Table 14.1) that shows the difference between starting a savings plans at different ages, and the amount each would need to invest annually to end up with the same amount net after tax. As you will note, the earlier you begin, the better.

Table 14.1 assumes 10 percent compounded interest. Net after tax assumes (account balance − principal) × .60 + principal.

Our couple: The Smiths are in their mid-forties. If they had not already started saving any substantial sums, they would have to save 2.5 times more than a couple in their mid-thirties, but they would be better off than those in their fifties, who would have to save 7.5 times more than those in their thirties.

The Smiths determine they will need at least $1 million in the bank at the time they retire. They will need to start saving $20,000 per year to accumulate enough to meet this retirement goal. Let's take a look at the Smiths' situation and see how they are doing.

Mark (46) and Cathy (43) currently earn a combined income of $150,000. They have been saving inside their 401(k)s for almost 10 years but have not been saving a substantial amount in retirement savings outside of that. Their kids are ages 15, 12, and 10, so saving for college has been of primary importance in their minds. They now have enough money saved for this—between 50 and 75 percent of the expected cost.

TABLE 14.1

Different Ages and Savings Rates

	Investor A Savings Rate	Investor A Savings Balance	Investor B Savings Rate	Investor B Savings Balance	Investor C Savings Rate	Investor C Savings Balance
35	2000	2000				
36	2000	4209				
37	2000	6650				
38	2000	9346				
39	2000	12325				
40	2000	15615				
41	2000	19251				
42	2000	23267				
43	2000	27703				
44	2000	32604				
45	2000	38018	5000	5000		
46	2000	44000	5000	10524		
47	2000	50606	5000	16626		
48	2000	57905	5000	23267		
49	2000	65969	5000	30813		
50	2000	74878	5000	39039		
51	2000	84717	5000	48128		
52	2000	95588	5000	58168		
53	2000	107597	5000	69258		
54	2000	120867	5000	81510		
55	2000	135520	5000	95045	15000	15000
56	2000	151710	5000	110000	15000	31570
57	2000	169597	5000	126516	15000	49877
58	2000	189360	5000	144763	15000	70101
59	2000	211184	5000	164921	15000	92439
60	2000	235297	5000	187195	15000	117119
61	2000	261935	5000	211792	15000	144383
62	2000	291370	5000	238970	15000	174505
63	2000	323873	5000	268993	15000	207773
64	2000	359787	5000	302167	15000	244530
65	2000	399461	5000	338800	15000	285135
Net	62000	264476	105000	245280	165000	237081

Detailed here is the outflow that is consistent with a net after-tax income of approximately $8100 per month:

Bills:

Mortgage:	$2,450	(Balance = $275,000 + taxes + insurance)
(2) Cars:	$ 670	(One leased, and one owing $18,000)
Utilities:	$ 300	(Gas, electric, cable, phone, water, garbage
Food:	$ 450	
Credit Card:	$ 0	(Balance of $0)
Clothing:	$ 300	
Life Insurance:	$ 125	(Term policies on each for $500,000)
Car Insurance:	$ 80	(Will go up when first child reaches 16)
Miscellaneous:	$ 400	
Total:	**$4,775**	

Savings:

(2) 401(k)s:	$1,239	(826 is 6 percent, assuming that employers match $0.50 on the dollar)
Mutual Funds:	$1,000	(earmarked for college education)
Total	**$2,239**	

Savings Balance:

(2) 401(k)s:	$189,000
Mutual Funds:	$ 54,000
Total	**$243,000**

In this situation, the Smiths have approximately $1500 per month left over after fulfilling their current savings rate. It is critical that the Smiths start saving for retirement. Let's look at what a variable annuity could do for them.

If the Smiths placed $5000 in a new variable annuity and contributed $1000 per month with an anticipated retirement at age 65, at 10 percent interest they would have $1,108,227. If annuitized and producing a guaranteed income for life, they would get a net investment income at 10 percent interest of $66,572 after tax at 65, and at age 80 that would grow to $136,945. This combined with their 401(k) savings, which should balloon to $2.3 million at 10 percent, should produce ample income to retire at the same lifestyle as they are currently enjoying, assuming current inflation rates.

Our suggestion here is for the Smiths to set up a variable annuity and contribute at least $1000 per month, which still affords them ample liquidity within their mutual funds and additional discretionary dollars of $500 per month.

IN YOUR FIFTIES: A CASE STUDY

Statistically, the majority of people in their fifties are watching their kids enter college or leave the nest. Typically, their children range in age from 15 to graduating college. The top issue of concern to this age group is, without question, retirement planning. The availability of funds for savings is usually much more substantial, assuming the kids' college expenses are covered and most major purchases, such as the purchase of a home, have been met. Financial suicide is too often experienced in this bracket due to the euphoria of having extra money now that the kids are on their own, and huge chunks of savings are sunk into new homes. That's usually not good long-term strategy for retirement.

If working past the age of 65 or 75 suits you, blow your savings and future retirement income on a palatial estate! Many in this age bracket do just the opposite, and they're financially independent and secure. My own parents sold everything and now live happily in a motor home traveling the country. This is extreme, but you should be thrifty at this point in your life, unless you have accumulated such significant wealth that you do not need advice on how to maximize your retirement income.

Another common mistake is not planning appropriately for life expectancy. With the average mortality rates increasing at a constant pace, you should plan on living to at least age 90. With this in mind, the next 10 years of savings will be critical; the prospect of guaranteeing income for life should be more dominant in your planning.

As illustrated earlier in Table 14.1, it is predicted that you will need to save approximately $60,000 per year for the next 15 years if you plan to have $1 million saved at retirement. This, however, is assuming you have no retirement savings today.

Let's take a look at Gary and Barbara Linderer's situation and see how they are doing.

The Linderers currently earn a combined income of $175,000. They have been saving inside their 401(k) plans for over 10 years and, in addition, have accumulated money inside mutual funds and a variable annuity. Their kids are out of college, and Gary and

Barbara plan to stay in their current house. The following shows the monthly outflow that is consistent with a net after-tax income of approximately $9200 per month.

Bills:

Mortgage:	$2,450	(Balance = $125,000 (10 yrs.) + taxes + insurance)
(2) Cars:	$ 540	(One owned outright, and one owing $10,000 (. . .0–2 yrs)
Utilities:	$ 300	(Gas, electric, cable, phone, water, garbage)
Food:	$ 250	
Credit Cards:	$ 0	(Balance of $0)
Clothing:	$ 250	
Life Insurance:	$ 175	(Term policies on each for $500,000)
Car Insurance	$ 80	
Miscellaneous:	$ 400	
Total:	**$4,445**	

Savings

(2) 401(k)s:	$ 1,950	(Each maximum funded up to the 1997 limit of $9500 + empl.)
Mutual Funds:	$1,000	
Variable annuity:	$1,000	
Total	**$ 3,950**	

Savings Balance:

(2) 401(k)s:	$265,000	
Mutual Funds:	$ 62,000	(What is left after college education)
Variable annuitiy:	$118,000	
Total	**$445,000**	

The Linderers have approximately $2000 per month left over after fulfilling their current savings rate. Since they have approximately 10 years until retirement, their current savings at 10 percent will be worth just shy of $2 million. In this case, additional savings would be an added bonus, not a requirement. They should have enough based on current savings and monthly deposits to live out a comfortable retirement. The important issue will be in about 10 years when income needs will require a critical decision about the variable annuity. We will address the annuitization advantage later in this book.

TABLE 14.2

Various Monthly Amounts Invested at 8 Percent

Years until Retirement	$100 Monthly Investment at 8%	$200 Monthly Investment at 8%	$300 Monthly Investment at 8%	$500 Monthly Investment at 8%
1	$1,251	$2,503	$3,754	$6,257
5	7,341	14,683	22,024	36,707
10	18,128	36,257	54,385	90,642
15	33,978	67,956	101,934	169,889
20	57,266	114,532	171,798	286,330
25	91,484	182,068	274,452	457,420
30	141,761	283,523	425,284	708,807
35	215,635	431,271	646,906	1,078,176
40	324,180	648,361	972,541	1,620,902
45	483,669	967,337	1,451,006	2,418,344

Assuming you are not as fortunate as the Linderers and do not have a substantial savings amount at 50-something, but you do have the same amount available to invest, let's look at what the variable annuity could do for you.

Table 14.2 shows how a monthly contribution builds the value of an account over time. *Use it for a quick reference when figuring out your own needs.*

The table assumes a hypothetical 8 percent average annual return. If an investor needs to have nearly $650,000 in his account when he retires, he should be saving $200 a month if he is 40 years from retirement. If an investor waits until 35 years from retirement, he would need to save $300 a month. Put another way, the earlier saver achieves his goal with a $96,000 investment ($200 × 12 × 40). The person who starts five years later must invest $126,000 ($300 × 12 × 35) to reach a similar target. This chart is for illustrative purposes only. It does not represent an investment in any particular fund.

IN YOUR RETIREMENT YEARS: RECOMMENDATIONS

The majority of clients we work with who are in their sixties are either retired or very close to it. For this reason, we will look at this age bracket as moving from the accumulation phase to the required income phase. This is a critical difference from the earlier examples, where the focus was on the planning aspect based on additional disposable dollars needed. Now we will focus on how to maximize dollars saved.

For those of us in our thirties and forties, the possibility of receiving a pension is minimal. The situation is very different for those who are now close to or beginning early retirement. Pensions were a staple of the retirement planning process just 20 years ago, as was social security. Therefore, in addition to pensions, social security has been factored into the following example for our couple, now in their mid-sixties.

Raymond and Phyllis Hutton have just retired. They are not looking to improve their lifestyle in retirement but rather to maintain their current status.

One advantage they have in moving from the career phase of life into the retirement phase of life is that certain expenses go away. The Huttons have religiously saved 15 to 20 percent of their income during the last few years, and they can now reduce their gross income in retirement by 15 to 20 percent without feeling the pinch.

The Huttons might also be able to eliminate business expenses such as lunch, gas, and parking from their balance sheet; but the fact is, many expenses don't stop just because you retire. And if you're active, you'll have significant new ones. These business-related dollars might be more realistically reallocated to hobbies, medical costs, or travel.

Maintaining your lifestyle in retirement, however, may nonetheless require a significantly lower amount of income. If you currently earn $100,000 combined and your net take-home pay after savings and taxes is approximately $56,000, when you retire you may need a gross income of only $80,000 to net the same amount. This is assuming that all of your income in retirement is taxable.

The beauty of the annuitization phase of the variable annuity is that a portion of your income will be returned to you as principal, which is free from taxation. If your income is structured properly, you may be able to maintain the $100,000 preretirement lifestyle on as little as $65,000 to $70,000 of income. This would involve a reduction of marginal tax rate from 31 percent to 28 percent. In that situation, you would be able not only to defer taxation of 31 percent during accumulation of the variable annuity but you would also eliminate 3 percent—the difference between accumulating at 31 percent and distributing at 28 percent.

This example is a conservative one. In some situations, people in the 39.6 percent federal tax bracket may be able to sustain the lifestyle they are currently accustomed to—if they have alleviated debt, have no additional savings needs, and do not have dependent children, with an income in the 28 percent bracket. Think about that for a second. In that situation, 11.6 percent of tax is eliminated, which is actually a 30 percent saving (11.6% ÷ 39.6%).

My recommendation for people in their sixties who are close to or in retirement, and who want to maximize retirement income, is to annuitize a large portion of their nonqualified dollars—and use the qualified dollars as their liquidity. Those who just recently purchased an annuity will be best suited to begin using their qualified funds first so as to allow the annuity to defer as long as possible.

Let's go back to our example. The Huttons are currently in the retirement phase and have two investments that were made outside of their qualified plan 15 years ago. They invested $100,000 into both a variable annuity and a mutual fund. At the time of accumulation, they were in a 31 percent federal tax bracket and a 28 percent capital gains bracket. Now in retirement, they are lowering their income which, in turn, has lowered their marginal tax bracket to 28 percent.

Let's assume the Huttons have never made distributions and received a 12 percent gross rate of return. The net return of the mutual fund is 11.3 percent, and the net return of the variable annuity is 10.65 percent—the difference being the cost of insurance for a no-load variable annuity. The accumulation graph would look like Figure 14.1

If at age 65 both of the Huttons tragically die, the net value of the variable annuity (assuming 100 percent of the growth would be taxed at the maximum rate to the heirs) would be $310,499. The step-up value (the amount passing to heirs as the new basis) of the mutual fund would be $336,034. If both of the Huttons die at age 85, the net value of the variable annuity passing to heirs would be $2,059,130, while the step-up value of the mutual fund would only be $1,754,276. The net value of the annuity would be $304,854 higher than the stepped-up benefit at death of the mutual fund. The

FIGURE 14.1

Accumulation

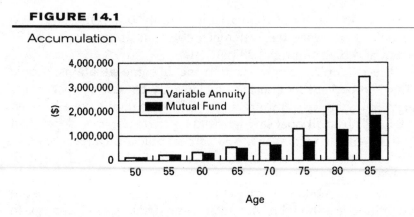

Age

money would also not go through probate, which would save both
time and approximately 5 percent of the value, which would otherwise go to attorneys—a savings of another $87,714.

In this case, the purchase of the annuity is the far better choice
for the heirs. Now what would be the best income option for the
Huttons to choose for their annuity? The answer by far is a life
annuitization with a period certain. Under this option, the insurance company guarantees that income will be received for the life
of the Huttons, and if one dies before the other, income will continue to the surviving spouse.

The disadvantage with the annuity is that the principal is not
accessible. Solution: Do not annuitize qualified plan money. If there
isn't any qualified plan money, keep a large amount of mutual fund
money—that has not yet been taxed—outside the annuity. Then
move the taxed money of the mutual fund into a single premium
immediate annuity.

If, instead of annuitizing, the Huttons attempted to use the
mutual fund on a systematic withdrawal perspective, the mutual
fund would run out of money completely if they lived beyond age
81. Compare this to an equal net after-tax distribution from the
variable annuitization, and there's no race.

The conclusion: Accumulate money inside a mutual fund or
variable annuity. If you have money that you can use for liquidity,
look to annuitize a portion of your other nonqualified funds as a
means of guaranteeing yourself income for life. In addition, if you

use a variable annuitization that performs greater than 4 percent, that will further increase your income for life.

If you have not accumulated funds in either a variable annuity or a mutual fund outside of your qualified plan, then I would recommend you think carefully about annuitizing your qualified plan. If you are a gambler and believe that you will outlive the current mortality tables, annuitize a portion of your qualified plan to assure yourself a guaranteed income for life. If you do not feel confident that you will outlive the mortality tables, do not even think about it. An exclusion ration is not an issue in a qualified plan, since all of the income would be taxable, so the break-even for the annuitization over the systematic withdrawal is age 85-plus.

In the next chapter, we will look at investment performance confusion. It is very difficult for consumers to believe everything they read, since many brokerage firms claim to have the number one mutual fund manager in the country. I hope to shed some light on this confusing topic.

Investment Performance Confusion

Anyone who has heard sales pitches about variable annuities from different stock brokerage firms will probably agree that there is a lot of confusion surrounding investment performance. It would appear that each brokerage house represents the number one manager in the country. How can this be? Everybody can't be number one, or can they?

There will be some period of time when a mutual fund or annuity sub-account will show top quartile performance of all mutual funds or sub-accounts in the country. Even a broken clock is right twice a day. The brokerage or mutual fund will pick the best time period to represent its performance.

Mutual funds, banks, brokers, insurance companies, and money managers use various methods to calculate investment returns. While the different approaches are usually perfectly legitimate, they can make comparisons difficult. One thing to keep in mind: Performance figures you see in brochures are there for one reason—marketing.

As an investor, however, you aren't helpless. You can either solicit help from an investment management consultant or take the time to get a better understanding of how performance is reported and how risk-and-return statistics work. In these ways, you can reduce the chance of falling victim to inflated sales pitches.

UNDERSTANDING RETURNS

If a manager shows that three years of returns on an investment portfolio totals 27 percent, did the investment earn 9 percent a year or 6.96 percent a year? Both answers, and numerous others, could be correct. How can this be?

The difference arises from the use of two types of return calculations. The simplest is the *average,* where the returns for any number of past periods are added up and divided by the number of periods.

The second calculation, more widely used by investment firms, is the *compound,* or annualized, rate of return. This figure is the rate at which $1 would have to grow in each of several periods to reach an ending amount.

Unlike the average, the compound return takes into account the sequence of earnings or losses. That's because a gain or loss in any one year directly affects the amount of money left to build up in subsequent years. Thus, a big gain in an earlier year generates a higher compound return than if the same gain had occurred more recently. In addition, the bigger the swings in returns from one period to the next, the lower the returns compared with average calculations.

Both average and compound return calculations can be useful in checking an investment's track record. The average return is going to give you some information about what is most likely to happen, but used together with the compound return, you also get the idea of the risk involved—so it's important to look at both.

TIME VERSUS DOLLAR WEIGHTING

While average and compound calculations produce different returns over several periods, the choice between so-called time-weighted and dollar-weighted calculations produces different return figures for the same period.

The dollar-weighted, or internal, calculation shows the change in value of a portfolio for the average funds invested in the period, including cash added or withdrawn by the investor. That sounds like it covers all the bases, but those cashflows can be a problem in calculating the true performance of the investment manager. Because the manager can't control the size and timing of money flow-ing in and out of an account, a time-weighted calculation can be used to figure the value of $1 invested for the entire period, eliminating distortions from cashflows.

For the question of how your investment manager is doing, you want a time-weighted return. For the question of how your money is doing, you might want to calculate the dollar-weighted rate of return.

Over short periods of, say, a month—or when there isn't any cashflow—the difference between time-weighted and dollar-weighted calculations usually isn't significant. But the difference grows in importance as time and cashflow increase.

Per-share values of mutual funds are calculated on a time-weighted basis. Returns for savings accounts paying a constant rate are the same whether calculated on a time-weighted or dollar-weighted basis.

VOLATILITY

It might appear that a 10 percent investment gain in one period, followed by a 10 percent loss the next period, would leave you no worse off than when you started—but the math doesn't work out that way. What first grew to $110, in this example, would shrink to $99 in the next period.

The distortion is greater with bigger numbers. A 50 percent loss on $100, followed by a 50 percent gain, leaves you with $75, still a long way from the original $100. In fact, after a 50 percent loss, a 100 percent gain is required to get back to the original $100 investment.

Such big swings reflect high volatility that can eat deeply into portfolio results over time. Cautious investment professionals continually warn that risk and returns are usually linked, as evidenced in the 1980s by the performance of the high-risk, high-yield junk bond market. A loss in just one year will put a dent in investment results for years to come, so it's well worth reviewing volatility as closely as returns.

By looking at only raw rates of return, you often have a very incomplete picture of why a manager earned what he did. The important thing to determine is the kinds of risk a manager took to get that rate of return. The Association for Investment Management and Research (AIMR) provides Performance Presentation Standards that can give you some insights into how the managers reported their results. These are a set of guiding ethical principles intended to promote full disclosure and fair representation in the reporting of investment results.

The objective of these standards is to ensure uniformity in reporting so that results are directly comparable among investment managers. To this end, some aspects of the standards are mandatory. These are listed in the box that follows. However, not every situation can be anticipated in a set of guidelines. Therefore, meeting the full disclosure and fair representation intent means making a conscientious good-faith interpretation of the standards consistent with the underlying ethical principles.

PERFORMANCE PRESENTATION STANDARDS

Association for Investment Management and Research (AIMR)

MANDATORY REQUIREMENTS

Presentation of total return using accrual is mandatory as opposed to cash-basis accounting. (Accrual accounting is not required for dividends, nor is it required for retroactive compliance.)

Time-weighted rate of return using quarterly valuation as a minimum time period (monthly preferred), and geometric linking of period returns is required.

Size-weighted composites are mandatory, using the beginning of period values to weight portfolio returns. (Equal-weighted composites are recommended as additional information, but are not mandatory.) Inclusion of all actual, fee-paying, discretionary portfolios in one or more composites within the firm's management is required. (No selectivity in portfolios, and no simulation or portability of results within composites is allowed.)

Presentation must be made of annual returns at a minimum for all years. (No selectivity in time periods is allowed.)

Inclusion of cash and cash equivalents in composite returns are mandatory.

MANDATORY DISCLOSURES

Prospective clients must be advised that a list of all of a firm's composites is available.

Continued

For each composite, disclosure of the number of portfolios, the amount of assets, and the percentage of a manager's total assets that are represented by the composite is required. For composites containing five or fewer portfolios, disclosure of composite assets, the percentage represented of the firm's total assets, and a statement declaring that the composite includes five or fewer portfolios is also required.

Historical compliance is at the discretion of the manager. When the firm's historical performance record is presented, a disclosure must be made that identifies the in-compliance periods from the periods that are not in compliance. The firm must also disclose that the full historical performance record is not in compliance. If semiannual or annual valuation periods are used to calculate returns and weight composites for retroactive compliance, this must also be disclosed.

Disclosure must be made of whether balanced portfolio segments are included in single-asset composites and, if so, how the cash has been allocated between asset segments. Disclosure of whether performance results are calculated gross or net of fees and inclusion of the manager's fee schedule in either case is required. Disclosure of whether leverage has been used in portfolios included in the composite and the extent of its usage is required. Disclosure of a settlement date valuation is required if used in place of a trade date. Disclosure must be made of any nonfee paying portfolios included in composites.

STRONGLY RECOMMENDED GUIDELINES AND DISCLOSURES

Re-evaluation of the portfolio is recommended whenever cash flow and market action combine to distort performance. (Cash flows exceeding 10 percent of the portfolio's market value often cause such distortions.) Methodology must be disclosed.

Standard deviation of composite returns across time or other risk measures as determined by the manager should be disclosed.

Comparative indices appropriate to the composite's strategies are relevant. Presentation of returns on a cumulative basis for all periods should be included. Median-sized portfolio and portfolio size range for each composite (unless five or fewer portfolios) are important.

Percentage of total assets managed in the same asset class as represented by the composite (for example, percentage of total equity assets managed) is relevant.

Continued

Trade date is preferred; settlement date is acceptable. One must be disclosed.

If leverage has been used, results on an all-cash (unleveraged) basis are provided where possible.

Convertible securities that are not reported separately are assigned to an asset class (equities, under most circumstances) and cannot be shifted without notice being given to clients concurrently or before such shifts.

Presentation of performance may be either gross or net of fee as long as the method is disclosed and the fee schedule is attached. AIMR prefers performance gross of fees.

Accrual accounting for dividends and for retroactive compliance is normal and acceptable.

Equal-weighted composites should be presented, in addition to the mandatory presentation of asset-weighted composites.

What happens when a manager uses the total return of a balanced composite to market a balanced account strategy?

When a manager uses the total return of a balanced composite to market balanced account strategy but wishes to present the portion of the balanced composite as supplemental information in presenting the balanced strategy, the segment returns can be shown without making a cash allocation as long as the returns for each of the composite's segments (including the cash portion or segment) are shown along with the composite's total return.

In fixed-income or other single-asset strategies, a cash allocation to each segment must be made at the beginning of the reporting period. For example, if a manager is using the equity-only returns of the equity portion of the balanced composite as an indication of expertise in managing equity-plus-cash portfolios, the manager must assign a cash allocation to the equity portion at the beginning of each reporting period. That segment can then be included on the firm's list of composites. For retroactive compliance, a manager must make a reasonable and consistent cash allocation to each of the composite segments and must disclose the methodology used for assigning cash.

When the results of the balanced segments are added to single-asset composites, a cash allocation needs to be made to each segment. This prevents a manager from mixing asset-without-cash returns to asset-plus-cash returns.

CHAPTER 16

Mistakes Most Investors Make

I regularly see the same mistakes made in regard to variable annuity investing. By pointing them out, I hope to help you avoid them.

MISTAKE 1: LISTENING TO THE FINANCIAL PRESS AS IF IT'S THE GOSPEL

What financial advisors explain in 250 pages, the media attempts to explain in 300 words. This does not mean that what the press writes is wrong; it is simply impossible for a writer, even a talented and well-respected one, to tell all sides of a story in such a short space. I know this for a fact because I received a call from such a writer to get feedback on a story she was writing about annuities. Although she admitted to the fact that she had not thought of things the way I described, what I said never made it to the papers. I do not blame that writer or anyone else for omissions that would shed light on a topic as complicated as this one. But that explains why, after completing this book, you will be far more educated than the majority of investors.

The financial media has had a field day announcing to information-hungry investors that the recent tax law changes will make variable annuities obsolete. If you were to rely solely on the headlines in the popular press, you would consider annuities dead now that capital gains taxes have been cut.

More astute investors, however, would have noticed *The Wall Street Journal*'s Monday section titled "Annuity Watch," which lists annuity companies, sub-accounts, prices, and the Lipper Annuity Indexes. That *Journal* column has grown to a full page. Astute investors should reason that savvy firms like Dow Jones aren't going to risk money on a dying market—*au contraire!*

Let's look at my friend's situation: At his request, every month an automatic contribution to a chosen variable annuity is deducted from his bank account. But the local newspaper advises him simply to buy the underlying mutual funds instead and pay the taxes, saying that he'll be better off. If he does that, he needs to know which of the capital gains tax rates apply to his investments. He's a financial journalist and well-organized, but now he's looking at having to analyze all his statements and figure out how long each investment in his mutual funds has been held. He needs to know if they were purchased 12 months ago, 18 months ago, 5 years ago, and so on. When tax time rolls around, he needs to keep his accountant in the loop on every single purchase and redemption. As if life isn't short enough!

The variable annuity is far easier and more efficient for my friend, the journalist. Whether the breakeven between a mutual fund or a mutual fund inside a variable annuity is 5, 10, or 15 years is virtually irrelevant to him. What's more important is what's going to be easy and save him time, while still providing a very high probability of retiring comfortably. Using the variable annuity, he doesn't have to report to his accountant until he receives the first distribution, years from now. But the main reason my friend chose a variable annuity in the first place was to help him accumulate additional assets. Outcome: He stuck with his original decision and his time is freed up to write.

MISTAKE 2: BELIEVING MUTUAL FUND RETURNS ARE ALL SUBJECT TO LONG-TERM CAPITAL GAINS

I just received my 1099DIV for 1997 and was very surprised to find that my investment gain was approximately $9000, but my dividends were about $8500. In addition, my capital gains that were distributed totaled another $3500. This is not going to happen every year; but when it does, it definitely emphasizes the need for tax-deferral. I will end up paying taxes on more income than I earned. This is because certain international holdings of mine had a negative return, but still paid dividends. When this happens, you lose twice!

Institutional investors, not taxable investors, heavily influence the stock market. One reason for this is that mutual fund managers are constrained by regulation to distribute virtually all dividends, interest, and realized capital gains in the year they are earned, and to carry net losses forward to offset future gains. (This is one reason why mutual funds have been called "the best thing that ever happened to the IRS.") Mutual fund managers often cannot avoid frequent trading, as they must respond to the investment and redemption requirements of fickle fund investors, regardless of the tax consequences. Aside from index funds, mutual fund managers employ very active day-to-day short-term trading to maximize total return.

This common approach takes away any advantage of the new lower capital gains tax rate and still leaves taxable investors exposed to nearly a 40 percent tax. The elimination of the "short-short" rule, which limited to 30 percent the amount of gain a mutual fund could realize from selling securities held less than 90 days, is likely to intensify this effect.

Deferring gains to future years, on the other hand, can focus variable annuity accounts on the after-tax return actualities, simply. It's not computer science. If a mutual fund is trading inside your variable annuity, you pay zero tax today—which enables your principal to compound tax-free. That's a far better deal.

MISTAKE 3: THINKING MUTUAL FUNDS ARE MORE FLEXIBLE THAN VARIABLE ANNUITIES

First, the owner of the annuity doesn't pay taxes on annuity interest until funds are paid out. Second, since an annuity does not pay out income or distribute any capital gains, the investor accumulates units that grow tax-deferred, making the compound effect even more dramatic. Third, unlike fixed-rate annuities where an insurance company determines how to invest funds, a variable annuity allows the investor to choose his or her own investments. These advantages can significantly enhance returns inside the wrapper of the variable annuity, allowing growth along with dividends.

But the most important benefit of all is the payout option that protects the investor's retirement savings. The primary goal of a retirement plan is to provide employees with a lifetime stream of retirement income. You may be surprised to learn that variable annuities were specifically created to satisfy that goal and were recognized by Congress to be a legitimate funding vehicle for qualified plans. This does not mean that I believe annuities should be used for everyone's IRA during accumulation, but during distribution they make sense if annuitized.

MISTAKE 4: BELIEVING ALL VARIABLE ANNUITIES HAVE HIGH SALES CHARGES

It's only fair to point out that consumers who do not do their homework in selecting the right variable annuity might possibly experience high sales charges, high surrender charges, and/or high administrative costs. In addition, some variable annuities only offer a limited array of mutual fund investment solutions. These drawbacks have generated some of the negative press about variable annuities.

While many annuities have high back-end surrender charges for early withdrawals, these charges and the length of time they apply to the policy vary widely across the industry. Back-end fees can run 6 to 7 percent the first year and usually decline one percentage point per year. Many annuities allow an annual withdrawal of up to 10 percent of the annuity value without any surrender charges. Some, though, have no company-imposed penalty for early withdrawal.

Mortality charges, ranging in the industry from 50 to 150 basis points, are the premiums paid to the insurance company that offers the annuity. Administrative charges range from 0 to 25 basis points. Portfolio costs vary widely from one annuity to another, even within the same portfolio of funds. Again, some annuities can cost even less than the mutual funds you now own.

The ideal variable annuity keeps its costs relatively low and eliminates up-front commissions. For example, consider the Federated Growth and Income Fund, which is handled by 50 different variable annuity companies. The return you'll get from that fund is

TABLE 16.1

Costs and Net Returns

Annuity	Gross Return	Mortality Cost	Portfolio Cost	Net Return
Annuity A	15%	140 bps	105 bps	12.55%
Annuity B	15%	85 bps	85 bps	13.3%
Annuity C	15%	65 bps	85 bps	13.5%

going to be the same regardless of which annuity it's in, except for the variance caused by insurance expenses. What you actually receive as a return, therefore, will be different based on differences in insurance expenses. The critical point here is that if the Federated Growth and Income Fund is one you want to use, it's an advantage to look at all the annuities that offer it to figure out which is the best deal. Also, check to see if there are any other funds that you want to use within the annuities you are considering.

How dramatic can the difference be? If the gross annual return of the Federated Fund for the last three years had been 15 percent and you had the choice of the three annuities in Table 16.1, which would you choose?

Based on data provided by Lipper Analytical Services, the total average cost difference between variable annuities and mutual funds in 1997 was only 67 basis points. This is because the underlying funds in variable annuities occasionally impose lower fees than publicly offered mutual funds, and those lower expenses offset the insurance charges to some extent. This is a crucial point when analyzing the costs and benefits of a variable annuity vis-à-vis a mutual fund. Lower fund expenses can offset almost half of the extra expense charges. But you won't read that in the newspapers.

FINANCIAL BLUNDERS

If you're like many conscientious investors, you probably want control of your finances. What you may fail to realize, however, is that you could be inadvertently hindering your investing potential by committing some major financial blunders. These common mistakes are not limited to inexperienced investors or those with moderate incomes; seasoned, sophisticated investors can be guilty, too. To help you recognize these errors so you can rectify them, here are seven major mistakes that many people make when handling their money.

1. Failing to Follow Through on Long-Range Goals

Many investors set up an investment plan but do not follow through by purchasing investments that satisfy their long-term objectives. Instead, they own a hodgepodge of investments bought on tips, hearsay advice, or casual comments from stockbrokers, financial advisors, and friends. Concentrate on those instruments designed to fulfill your financial plan.

2. Failing to Follow a Balanced Investment Program

Diversify into bonds and equities. This helps lessen the overall risk in your portfolio, because it balances your investments' gains and losses, while shielding your portfolio from economic downturns.

Customize your portfolio to reflect your objectives and your ability to assume risk. If you're a stock investor who likes to invest exclusively in one industry or sector, you may wish to consider abandoning this practice and, instead, diversify in several. This can help reduce vulnerability to certain crosscutting variables, such as government policies or consumer preferences.

3. Falling in Love with One's Own Investments

Be disciplined and regularly weed out the poor performers in your portfolio. You can accomplish this by reviewing individual stocks at least once a year and making it a goal to sell one that has performed poorly.

To take the emotion out of purchasing mutual funds or individual stocks, you could use a mechanical means such as dollar cost averaging that demands a specified contribution on a regular basis, regardless of market conditions. You can also set downside measures of price that trigger you to automatically sell regardless of your intuition. The extra advantage is that selling losers gives you the ability to offset gains from your winners. I do not however recommend this for annuity investments. You have to give these vehicles years for the tax deferral to pay off.

4. Chasing the Next "Hot" Mutual Fund

Chasing the next hot stock fund or funds can set you up for an emotional roller-coaster ride. Let me explain: Before I started following a sound strategy, I used to get a lot of "hot tips." My strategy at the time was not to act on them, but I would start following the "hot tip" in the newspaper. Sometimes the price moved up as was promised, but I still wouldn't buy. I would hope the tip would continue to go up so I could see a trend developing. If the stock kept moving up, my emotions would change to greed. Once greed struck, I would buy it.

What happened next? You're right! As soon as I bought it, it immediately went down. That sent my emotional state into fear that it would go lower and I would have to tell my wife how stupid I was. And yes, that's exactly what the hot tip most often did, it continued going down. Down until panic set in and I had to sell it for a loss.

I'm sure everyone knows someone this has happened to. As soon as I sold the hot stock for a significant loss, some new information would be announced and the stock would turn around and hit an all-time high. Then I would experience the feeling of disappointment for not waiting a little longer and not being smarter. The problem was I had no plan to keep me on track.

5. Failing to Keep Detailed Records of Investments, Loans, and Taxes

Many investors fail to keep accurate financial records because they simply don't bother or are too unorganized. Make the effort. It can help you monitor your investments' performance as well as aid your heirs after you're gone. Keep records of all your assets in a safe deposit box so your survivors have ready access to them.

6. Failing to Use Professional Advisers

Unless you have broad experience and plenty of spare time, you may save in the long run by obtaining professional help. Advisors such as bank investment representatives, financial planners, accountants, and tax attorneys can help you build and implement a comprehensive financial plan.

7. Failing to Take Time

The common theme that can be found in the writings of investment masters is *time*. A wise bank investor who gives his investments time will find the odds of winning on his or her side. But, for the most part, such sage and simple advice falls on deaf ears. If an investor invests where the odds are against him and time is not on his side, investing begins to look more like buying a lottery ticket.

These are not the only mistakes and blunders that investors make, but they are the majority. Avoiding the mistakes will be easier now that you're aware of them.

PART THREE

Structuring a "Guaranteed Income for Life"

CHAPTER 17

Defining the Distribution Phase Options

The distribution phase is the period that begins when you start taking payouts from your annuity. As you receive your investment earnings, you must pay federal income taxes on them. Sorry. But the good news is you've had Uncle Sam's money to build additional wealth, and one would hope you did a good job. Although that means you have more money to pay tax on, you may be in a lower income tax bracket when you begin distributions. If that is the case, you not only deferred taxes but eliminated a portion of them.

A variable annuity offers a wide range of payout options, and many investors choose to keep control of how their assets are paid out. You can take the entire value of the annuity in a single lump sum, or you can withdraw money just as you need it, or you can set up the annuity to make regular monthly payments to you until your assets are used up.

If you are willing to give up access to your principal, you can *annuitize* your investment. This means your annuity will be used to provide you, or someone you select, with periodic payments that the insurance company promises will last for either a certain number of years or for your lifetime. Once you do annuitize your investment, you may not change your decision after the annuity payments begin. Annuitization benefits have greatly changed in recent years and will be further explained in this chapter. The great news is that some companies allow you to continue to manage your portfolio while the annuitization stream is being paid out. This is a dramatic improvement over the fixed annuitization options available in the past.

BENEFIT PAYMENTS FROM VARIABLE ANNUITIES

When the time comes to receive the benefit payments from a variable annuity, the annuity holder must decide what portion of the payments he or she wishes to receive as a fixed annuity and what portion as a variable annuity. Depending on the contract, some insurance companies will not allow you to retain funds inside the variable options during annuitization. It is critical to ask that question of your carrier since the difference in future income could be dramatic.

A fixed annuity benefit payout simply means the benefit will be calculated and paid to the annuity holder in a manner similar to that used with a fixed annuity. At the time that benefit payments are to commence, all funds in a variable annuity are transferred into a general account of the insurance company. The insurance company agrees to pay an annuity that will not vary in amount from one payment to the next. This would be true whether the insurance company's investment returns are better or worse; the payments to the beneficiary would remain the same.

The main problem here is that the majority of fixed annuitization benefits are credited with a 3 percent or 4 percent investment return. Therefore I would avoid fixed annuitizations unless you are extremely risk averse.

Under the variable annuity payment payout, the annuity holder would not receive a check for the same amount each month. To understand this better, you need to understand the concept of annuity units. An annuity unit is a unit of measure used to determine the value of each income payment made under the variable annuity option. How the value of one unit is calculated is a fairly complicated process involving certain assumptions about investment returns. For example, Ms. Carter is entitled to a monthly benefit payment based on 100 annuity units each month. The amount of the payment would differ from month to month according to investment results of the investment accounts or sub-accounts. More specifically, if the dollar value of the annuity unit was $12 in the first month, Ms. Carter's benefit payments would be equal to 12 times the 100 units, which would be $1200. The following month, if the units rose to $12.50, Ms. Carter's payment would increase to $1250 (100 units × $12.50). In the following months, if the annuity value decreased to $11, Ms. Carter would receive the benefit check of $1100 (100 units × $11). Not all annuity holders are comfortable with this, and some like to split the difference between the fixed and variable approaches. The first payment of a variable annuitization is typically based on an assumed rate of 4 percent. If subsequent payment checks you receive are greater than the initial check, you know you did better than an annuitized 4 percent that month—and if less, you did worse.

Most annuity contracts will allow the annuity holder to place a portion of the accumulated value in the payout phase and allow the remainder to be diversified among the guaranteed general account and separate accounts. To illustrate, let's assume Ms. Carter's variable annuity contract has a total accumulation value of $500,000. She chooses to receive an income from half of this amount in a fixed account; thus, $250,000 is transferred to the insurance company's general account and annuitized. As a result, Ms. Carter is going to receive a hypothetical monthly benefit of $1600. Assuming she elects the life annuity settlement option, the benefit amount would come to her each month for the rest of her life, regardless of the investment returns the insurance company receives. The other $250,000 remains in a variable annuity investment account and continues to grow. This option allows Ms. Carter to receive a guaranteed income for life from a portion of her assets and retain liquidity from the other half.

Immediate Annuity

An immediate annuity begins paying benefits quickly, usually within one year of the time of purchase. It is usually a single-premium annuity. These immediate annuities are most often purchased by recipients of large sums of money: inheritance, settlement, lottery winnings, or the sale of a business. For example, Mr. Jones sold his business. He received a lump-sum payment of $100,000 and purchased a single-premium annuity that would provide him with a monthly income. If he elected a settlement option based on his life expectancy, he could have an income that he could not outlive. If the sale of the business is Mr. Jones's only asset, he should not annuitize all of it. He would be better off annuitizing a portion and keeping enough liquid to meet unexpected daily demands. Annuitizations are powerful but can be dangerous for those without careful liquidity planning.

Age at which Benefit Payments Begin

When do you need to take an annuitization? Well, the good news is that there is no age at which distributions or benefit payments must begin for a nonqualified annuity, which is not true for other types of investments, such as IRAs. However, most insurance companies specify the maximum age at which an annuity holder must begin to receive benefits paid out from the annuity. Like other annuity provisions, the maximum age varies in many contracts.

For some insurance companies, payments begin automatically when annuitants reach age 80 or 85 unless the annuitant declares that he or she does not wish to receive the income. Some annuities allow payments and benefits to be postponed past age 100. Other annuities, IRAs, and tax-sheltered annuities (TSAs) must begin making distributions of at least a minimum amount in the year following the year in which the individual reaches age $70\frac{1}{2}$. This is yet another benefit of the annuity funded with after-tax dollars. You are not forced into taking distributions that you do not want to receive.

Here Are Your Two Main Investment Choices during Annuitization:

1. If you choose a variable payment option, your assets would remain invested in the portfolios you select, and your periodic payments would vary, depending on the performance of those investments. If they perform well, your periodic payments could go up. But if they do poorly, your income could fall.
2. Under a fixed payment plan, your assets would be transferred into the general account of the insurance company, which would promise to make equal payments

to you for a specific period, such as the duration of your lifetime.

Okay, you understand the fact that you can do a fixed or a variable annuitization. This is just the first step. The following will outline the various payment options you can select once you make the decision to receive the income as either fixed or variable.

PAYMENT OPTIONS

The payment (or settlement) option is simply the method the annuity owner selects to receive payments of benefits under the annuity contract. The selection can be made when a contract is purchased or delayed until the time benefit payments are to start. Most annuity contracts allow the payment option to be changed with notice to the insurance company.

Following are the payment options:

1. Life annuity
2. Life with period certain
3. Refund life annuity
4. Joint survivor life annuity
5. Fixed-period annuity
6. Fixed-amount annuity
7. Interest-only option
8. Lump-sum payment

Life Annuity

If the annuitant elects the life annuity option, he or she receives payments until death. This would be true if the annuitant dies in the first year or after payments have been received for more than 30 years. This settlement option is the purest form of insuring that the annuitant does not outlive his or her financial assets. To illustrate the life annuity, let's use our example of the Carters. When Mr. Carter is 50 years of age, he decides to receive payments from his variable annuity under the life annuity option. Let's say he's accumulated a value of $200,000; his monthly payments for a variable annuitization would start at $1137. If he only requested 4 percent on his investment, he would receive that amount each month until his death. If he lives only to age 55, he would receive $68,220 in benefits; the difference of $131,780 ($200,000 less $68,220) will be lost to his heirs. On the other hand, if he lives to age 90, he would receive $1137 each month and collect a total of $545,760 in benefits, significantly in excess of the annuity's accumulated value of $200,000.

Just to show you the value of the variable annuitization, if he had received a 10 percent growth rate on his investments for five years, his benefit would have been $77,152, or $8932 more than the fixed annuitization benefit. Over the course of his lifetime, until his death at age 90, the total benefit received as income during a variable annuitization with 10 percent growth would have been $1,570,586, or nearly three times the fixed benefit. In the next chapter, we will analyze the payouts from different annuitization benefits.

Summary: The annuitant is guaranteed a lifetime income. At the death of the annuitant, all payments cease and the annuity is without value. No minimum number of payments is guaranteed.

Advantage: Payments are maximized for the life of the annuitant.

Disadvantage: At the annuitant's death, the annuity has no value to his or her beneficiary (estate).

Life with Period Certain

Life with period certain is a hedge against the loss of value if the annuitant dies shortly after the contract is annuitized. Under this option, the insurance company agrees to pay the annuity benefit for the longer of either the annuitant's lifetime or a certain period of years. Most insurance companies offer a choice of period certain, such as 10, 15, or 20 years. If the guaranteed period exceeds the life expectancy of the annuitant, then the benefit is assumed to be a period certain without life expectancy risk.

Back to our example of Mr. Carter, age 50. If he decides to annuitize his variable annuity contract for $200,000 under a life with 5-year certain settlement option, his monthly benefit would be approximately $1125. With a life with 10-year certain, his monthly benefit would be approximately $1110. Electing a life with 15-year certain, his benefit would be approximately $1095. Selecting a life with 20-year certain option, the benefit would be approximately $1050. The difference represents the amount of money the insurance company keeps to guarantee the risk of the annuitant dying prematurely. To many, a lower monthly benefit is worth the security of a 20-year guarantee. Let's say Mr. Carter selected the life with 20-year certain settlement option at age 50, but he only lived to age 65. His beneficiaries would receive the monthly payments of $1050 each month for the next five years, the remainder of the period certain. On the other hand, if he lived to age 72 (longer than the period certain), the annuity payments would cease at his death and his beneficiaries would not receive any payments from the annuity contract. This particular life with period certain provides excellent options for financial planning situations where there are a set number of years for a particular benefit a client desires.

Summary: The annuitant receives a lifetime income but a minimum number of payments are made whether the annuitant lives or dies. The annuitant receives two guarantees: A certain amount will be paid periodically for the lifetime of the annuitant; and should the annuitant die prior to the time-certain guarantee being satisfied (usually 5 to 20 years), the annuitant's beneficiary will receive the remaining number of guaranteed payments.

Advantages: The annuitant will receive a lifetime income. A minimum number of periodic payments will be made.

Disadvantages: The longer the guaranteed payments, the less the periodic payment. Beneficiary payments stop after the guaranteed time payment.

Refund Life Annuity

Refund life annuity is similar to the life with period certain guaranteed option. It's a hedge against the possibility of early death. Under the refund life annuity settlement option, the insurance company will pay a monthly benefit for the life of the annuitant. At the annuitant's death, if the amount that was applied to the annuitization of the contract is more than the total of installment payments received by the annuitant during his or her lifetime, the difference is paid in a lump sum to the beneficiaries.

For example, Mrs. Carter, also age 50, purchases a single-premium nonqualified annuity with $200,000 in it. Her monthly annuity payments under the refund life annuity settlement option are $876. Since Mrs. Carter is guaranteeing that her annuitized balance will be paid out regardless of age at death, her payments will be smaller than Mr. Carter's. If she lives to age 55, she'll receive an annuity value totaling $52,560. And since she elected the life refund annuity option, Mrs. Carter's beneficiaries receive a lump sum paid from the insurance company of $147,440 (the difference between $200,000 and $52,560).

However, if Mrs. Carter lives to be 85 and collects annuity payments for 35 years, she would receive a total of $367,920. As that amount exceeds her annuity value of $200,000, her beneficiaries would not receive anything upon her death.

Summary: The annuitant receives a lifetime income while protecting his or her heirs from losing the unused value of the amount annuitized. If premature death occurs, the heirs receive a lump sum.

Advantages: The annuitant will receive a lifetime income. The principal balance will also be guaranteed to be paid out if death occurs prematurely.

Disadvantage: The monthly income is reduced due to the higher risk to the insurance company of returning all funds not paid out during annuitization.

Joint Survivor Life Annuity

Under the joint survivor life annuity, the insurance company will pay benefits during the joint lifetimes of two individuals. Often the two people are husband and wife, although there's no requirement that it be that way. They do have to be individuals, not a trust or corporation, since these do not have a life expectancy. Under the joint survivor life annuity option, the insurance company pays the full benefit amount until the death of one of the annuitants. If the settlement option is a full joint survivor annuity, the payment will continue in the full amount until the death of the surviving annuitant. Under a joint and one-half survivor annuitant settlement option, payments are made in full until the death of one of the annuitants, but then reduced to one-half the full amount until the death of the survivor. Some insurance companies offer a joint with two-thirds survivor annuity in which the payments of the surviving annuitant are equal to two-thirds of the original full payment amount.

Let's say the Carters have accumulated $200,000 in their variable annuity. Electing the joint and full survivor annuity settlement option will result in a benefit of $854 paid to both Mr. and Mrs. Carter until the death of one of them—again, a further reduction in initial monthly benefit due to the longer life expectancy of two people. After the first death, the same amount of $854 would continue to be paid to the survivor until his or her death. If they elected the joint and one-half survivor settlement option, the amount paid to both of them would be approximately $865 until the first death, then the survivor would receive one-half the benefit, or $433 each month, until his or her death.

Electing the joint and two-thirds survivor settlement option, the Carters would receive a benefit of $860 until the first death, at which time the survivor would receive two-thirds, or $573, in benefit payments.

Summary: Periodic payments are guaranteed for the lifetimes of two or more annuitants. Payments continue until the death of the last annuitant. A husband and wife seeking a guaranteed joint lifetime income and then a guaranteed life income for the surviving spouse typically use the joint-and-last-survivor option. Periodic payments are made for the life of one person until his or her death. At that point, the survivor becomes the annuitant and payments are made until the death of the survivor. The periodic payments to the surviving annuitant may be less (three-fourths to one-half of the initial amount, depending on the survivor option).

Advantage: The annuitants are guaranteed a lifetime income.

Disadvantages: The periodic payment amount is less for two or more annuitants. The periodic payment may be reduced for the surviving annuitant(s).

Fixed-Annuity Period

The fixed-period payment option is probably the easiest to explain. This option allows the annuitant to receive the accumulated value of the annuity over a set number of years. For example, Mr. Carter, the annuity owner, age 50, may choose to annuitize his contract and receive the benefits over a 15-year period. He would be age 65 and eligible for Social Security, plus the benefits from any retirement plans, when his annuity payments end. Most companies offer a fixed-period payment option for periods of any length, from 5 years to 25 years.

Caution: If you choose a fixed-period annuitization from an existing contract and you have accumulated earnings that have not been taxed, the receipt of these earnings may be subject to a 10 percent federal penalty. One way to avoid the penalty if you need income prior to age $59\frac{1}{2}$ is to select a life contingency annuitization. In most cases the IRS allows this option to bypass the 10 percent federal penalty since you are receiving income for your lifetime.

Let's consider the annuity of Mrs. Carter, which has an accumulated value of $200,000; she decides to annuitize and elects the fixed-period payment option over a five-year period. Her monthly benefits would be $3664. She would receive this benefit payment each month for 60 months, or five years. At the end of this time, benefit payments would cease. No further funds would remain in the annuity contract and no further benefits would be payable. Again, the problem is that her gain would be taxable and a 10 percent federal penalty may be added. If Mrs. Carter should die during the five-year period, benefit payments would continue to her beneficiaries until the end of the fifth year.

Summary: This is a safe income option to choose for assuring the payout of the principal value. The benefit of guaranteed income for life is lost as are tax benefits such as the ability to start prior to age $59\frac{1}{2}$.

Advantage: The income can be substantially higher since the typical payout is for less than life expectancy.

Disadvantages: Unlike life contingency options, the payments are not tax-favored. With life contingency options, you receive principal with interest, which increases your net income. With a period certain, you receive interest first and you may be subject to a 10 percent federal penalty.

Fixed-Amount Annuities

Under the fixed-amount payment option, the annuitant receives benefit payments for a set amount until the annuity accumulation value, plus interest, runs out. Back to our example. Mr. Carter has an accumulated value of $200,000. Under this payment option, he could elect to receive a monthly benefit of $3000, or any amount he would prefer. The insurance company would send him a check each month for as long as the accumulated value and interest supports the benefit. After the funds in the annuity are exhausted, Mr. Carter will not receive any further benefits from the contract. In the event of his death, any funds remaining in the annuity are generally paid to the beneficiaries. This is more commonly referred to as a systematic withdrawal. In addition to a fixed-amount option, you can also choose a fixed-percentage option. For instance, you could say that you want 10 percent of the current balance every year. If your balance declines, so will your income; if your balance increases, so will your income.

Advantage: You do not give up access to your principal. Since you have not annuitized, you can access your account for additional distributions for unexpected events.

Disadvantages: Unlike life contingency options, the payments are not tax-favored. With life contingency options, you receive principal with interest, which increases your net income. With a systematic withdrawal, you receive interest first and you may be subject to a 10 percent federal penalty. In addition, some annuities may penalize you if you take distributions in excess of 10 percent of your account balance during the early years.

Interest Only Option

The interest only option is just what it says. If Mr. Carter had $200,000 and in 1998 received a net rate of return of 10 percent, he would receive $20,000 that year, which would be fully taxable; if received prior to age $59\frac{1}{2}$, the full amount may be subject to a 10 percent federal penalty. Those who do not want to withdraw income against principal most commonly choose this option.

Advantage: you have access to your income for rainy days.

Disadvantages: The income is fully taxable and can vary significantly. In down years, the income could be zero.

Lump-Sum Payment

The annuitant has the option of receiving the entire value of an annuity in a lump sum. This allows the annuitant to accumulate his or her funds in a tax-deferred manner and, if older than 59½ withdraw the funds without federal penalty. These assets could then be used for projects or starting a business.

Advantages: The annuitant retains complete control of the annuity value. The total account balance can be liquidated.

Disadvantages: The annuitant is not guaranteed a lifetime income. There may be tax and penalty consequences.

BENEFITS VERSUS CHARGES AND PENALTIES

The variable annuity offers many other benefits in addition to tax deferral. One of the most important is payout options, or *annuitization*, which helps retirees solve the income problem by guaranteeing a stream of payments that will continue for the rest of their lives, no matter how long that is. This advantage remains largely unrealized by the public because the popular press largely ignores the annuitization feature, with more focus being placed on the need to accumulate money for retirement. Additionally, most investors and their advisers fail to realize that the death benefit feature, as covered in Part One of this book, has a real practical meaning for most variable annuity buyers.

Obviously, no one can predict if he or she will die when the market is up or down. But, the *standard* death benefit provided by variable annuities guarantees that if the policyholder dies while still saving for retirement, his or her heirs will receive the greater of either the amount of money invested or the policy's value at the time of death. Many variable annuities go even further and offer "stepped up" benefits that actually lock in investment gains every year. If you die prior to being able to choose an annuitization option, this benefit can greatly protect your heirs.

It's important to read the annuity contract regarding free withdrawal provisions before taking a distribution. The requirements vary from contract to contract, and some companies credit a potential lower rate of interest on funds that are surrendered out of the contract than would have been credited if they'd remained in the contract.

Free withdrawal provisions, however, do not release the contract holder from income tax consequences, including the 10 percent premature distribution penalty tax. The contracts impose a surrender charge if the funds are removed from the contract by either a full or partial surrender within that certain number of years after the annuity contract is first purchased. In some contracts, the charges decline sharply from year to year and eventually no longer apply.

The point here is not to confuse the surrender charges, if your annuity contract has them, with the 10 percent penalty tax imposed by the Internal Revenue code on premature distribution, which was set up to discourage the use of annuity contracts as short-term tax-sheltered investments. A 10 percent tax is imposed on certain premature payments under the annuity contract. The 10 percent tax applies to the portion of any payment that is taxable. For example, if the annuity contract is surrendered for $50,000 and only $30,000 of the amount is included in the income of the owner of the contract, the 10 percent penalty applies only to the $30,000. Thus, the amount of the penalty tax is $3000. The contract's surrender charges apply during the first few years after the annuity is purchased, yet the individual may incur both the penalties depending on the circumstances.

CHAPTER 18

Analyzing the Payouts

Now that you have an understanding of all of the income options available in a variable annuity, how do you choose the best one for you?

How soon the retirement assets will be needed for income distributions will have a major impact on these comparisons. There are different distribution strategies available with variable annuities that can help maximize the tax benefits and total yield.

If you can invest for a minimum of 10 years prior to withdrawing retirement income, the variable annuity provides a tax-deferral advantage on earnings, payout options, and potential for higher investment returns, as well as insurance protection for your beneficiaries. However, if you are less than 10 years from needing income distributions, the costs and less favorable taxation of the annuity may negate the benefits of the tax deferral and the death benefit. If you have other sources of capital to use initially for retirement income, such as a 401k, you could defer any payout from the variable annuity for a sufficient period to maximize its benefits.

If you are using mutual funds, the implications of how to take distributions can set your mind spinning. Let's assume you're a disciplined investor who has held the funds for an extended period of time, receiving the beneficial compounding effect I illustrated earlier. There are now several relevant issues to consider, such as which shares should be sold, how long those shares were held, and whether you have records that can prove the holding period. There are now four different tax rates on investment income based on holding periods: ordinary tax rate (0–12 months); capital gains of 28 percent (12–18 months); capital gains of 20 percent (18–60 months); and capital gains of 18 percent (60+ months). It is a safe bet that you will never experience the 18 percent gains rate for a five-year holding period, since it is likely that capital gains rates will change before the five years are up. Additionally, you would incur a substantial tax liability and dilute your retirement income if you accumulated your savings within mutual funds, cashed them in, and bought an income annuity with the lump sum.

An alternative is to accumulate funds inside the variable annuity and annuitize the contract. This strategy enables you not only to defer the taxes during accumulation, but also to spread the tax on the deferred amount over the course of your life.

How to withdraw your funds is a very complex problem and it is impossible to cover all the variables. In the optimum scenario at retirement, the investor's mortgage is either paid or is within the reasonable limit of 1.5 times income. In addition, the investor has no other long-term debt, has a substantial amount saved in qualified retirement programs, has sufficient liquidity, and has accumulated a significant amount of money inside nonqualified investment vehicles.

Figure 18.1 illustrates what would happen if an individual chose to withdraw income from the account as a systematic withdrawal of 10 percent of the annuity value rather than in one lump sum.

Assuming the investor accumulated funds for 30 years and then started equal net distributions, the systematic withdrawal from an annuity or mutual fund provides him or her with an equal net after-tax income of $119,067. The problem in this situation for the investor who chooses to take systematic withdrawals from the mutual fund is that the money will run out in later years.

In Figure 18.2, the situation is a 35-year-old investor accumulating funds until age 65, then making withdrawals until age 90. Notice that the higher income is paid out at later ages by the annuitization, and that the mutual fund again runs out of money. This is a dramatically different income stream from that received as a systematic withdrawal, since the annuity income under

FIGURE 18.1

Distribution Period
(10% Systematic Withdrawal)

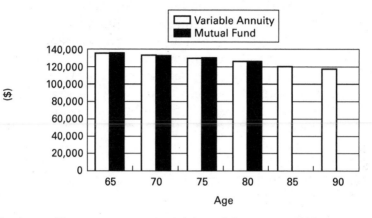

Distributions at 10 percent systematic withdrawals between variable annuities and mutual funds.

FIGURE 18.2

Distribution Period
(Life Annuitization)

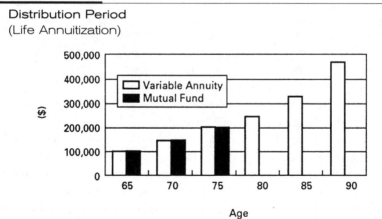

Distribution life annuitization.

annuitization rules is tax favored and increases due to the fact that the rate of return is a net 10.2 percent, which is higher than the 4 percent IRR (Initial Rate of Return).

These comparisons assume that the mutual fund was bought and not sold prior to distributing the annuitization. The results would be even more alarming in the case of an investor accumulating money inside a mutual fund and cashing it in to purchase an annuitization. Since the net amount invested in the annuitization would be far less due to taxation, the income would also be less.

If the investor took equal net distributions, as illustrated, and the annuity had more money at the start due to the mutual fund being liquidated, taxed, and reinvested as an annuitization, the distributions from the mutual fund would be reduced compared to the distributions from the annuity.

As if this argument isn't strong enough, consider the investor who dies at age 50 and had elected the systematic withdrawal option. The annuity would pay his beneficiaries $1,816,433, whereas the mutual fund would provide them with exactly $0. Remember, this is assuming a mid-thirties investor with an original investment of $100,000.

So, what's the catch? The catch is that if you were to take the annuitization option, you would not have access to the principal for emergency expenses. You can change your investment allocation to provide for less or greater risk in hopes of greater investment returns and a higher income, but unlike with a mutual fund, you cannot tap into the annuity for money when needed. The simple solution is not to annuitize all of your liquid assets. Keep enough money available for emergencies outside annuitizations.

Proper planning is necessary for the distribution option, just as for the accumulation options. If you think it is too soon to be thinking about these issues, think again. If you were to die prematurely with an annuitization and did not elect a period certain or refund option to guarantee additional payments after death, your beneficiaries could end up with nothing. Take the time to make sure you've addressed this.

In Figure 18.3, I have illustrated three of the income options you can select from an annuity to give you an idea of the various income levels you could receive. The calculations are based on the variables in Table 18.1.

FIGURE 18.3

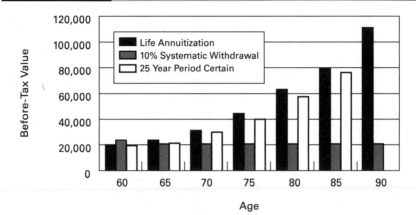

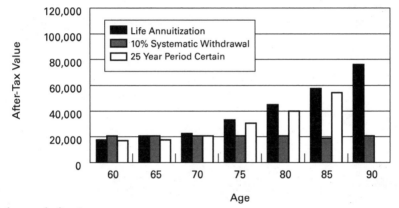

Before and after taxes.

TABLE 18.1

Different Income Options

Variables	Gross Income	Net Income
Current age	50	50
Age at withdrawals	60	60
Deposit	$100,000	$100,000
Deposit	$100,000	$100,000
Gross investment return	12%	12%
Cost of annuity	.65%	.65%
Cost of portfolio	.75%	.75%
Federal tax rate	28%	28%
State tax rate	6%	6%
Maximum capital gains rate	20%	20%
Income	Before taxes	After taxes

What you will notice is that the systematic withdrawal option has the initial advantage of providing you with additional income for the first few years. As time goes on, the life annuitization option is a far superior choice for keeping pace with inflation as well as providing you with an income that is guaranteed to be paid for as long as you live.

PART FOUR

Analysis, Selection, and Purchase of Annuities

CHAPTER 19

How to Find the Best Annuities

How do you define the "best" variable annuity? Many people identify the top-selling company as the one offering the best variable annuity. Others claim that the variable annuity distributed by the highest quality insurance carrier is the best. Some look to the biggest money managers, equating the largest with the best. Some purely look at cost and assume the cheapest is the best. Still others, some of the less professional commission brokers, view the variable annuity with the highest compensation to the selling broker/dealer as the best in the industry. With all these different points of view, the "best" can take on many meanings. Defining the "best" variable annuity is impossible because no one variable annuity can please all the potential buyers (and their advisors) all the time.

Studies show that today's best mutual funds end up as tomorrow's losers. This is not the case with variable annuities but may be the case with the sub-accounts within them. The secret is to do your homework, find a low-cost provider, get help from an advisor, and not purchase the first one thrown at you by a broker, who may earn up to a 7 percent commission if you buy it.

I have included in the appendix an extensive list of variable annuity companies. New players jump in daily so it is hard to keep up with everyone. I would recommend contacting a few companies and asking a series of questions that I outline in this chapter.

COMPANY RATINGS

Question: What are the ratings of your insurance company from A.M. Best, Standard & Poor's, Moody's, and Duff & Phelps?

The first criterion is the insurance company's ratings of strength and stability. Standard & Poor's, Duff & Phelps, A.M. Best, and Moody's Investor Services all rank insurance companies in terms of safety.

Some advisors who work for an insurance company or brokerage firm have their own in-house variable annuity products and may have a conflict of interest in recommending those products because of a higher payout. It behooves you to do independent research before going to broker.

Ratings of the insurance company are not as important for variable annuities as they are for fixed annuities. You are paying, however, for certain benefits that are guaranteed by the underlying company, and if you annuitized the contract, the solvency will be important.

Look for ratings that are at least A+ from A.M. Best, AA from Standard & Poor's, and A1 from Moody's. If ratings are lower than this, move on.

NUMBER OF INVESTMENT OPTIONS AND MONEY MANAGERS

Question: How many fund options do you make available inside your variable annuity? How many asset classes does this represent?

How much diversification and/or how many asset classes (i.e., international portfolios, sector portfolios, and other specialty portfolios) is sufficient for you as an investor? Do you need multiple-niche managers or is one large, broad-based, well-diversified money manager more appropriate for you? What you should be looking for here is a sufficient number of funds to choose from that represent at least the major asset classes. The major asset classes as I see them are U.S. large cap, U.S. small cap, international large cap, international small cap, and fixed income. If a phone query reveals that these asset classes are not available, hang up and move on.

DEATH BENEFITS

Question: What are your death benefit options and how much do they cost?

Death benefit options, as described in Part One, can be numerous. Only a few seem to make much sense to me for the price you have to pay.

To review the death benefit: If the annuitant dies, the value of the death benefit is the greater of the amount originally invested in the contract or the annuity's account value. The death benefit is guaranteed never to be lower than the amount invested in the annuity minus withdrawals.

If the annuity holder (investor) dies during the so-called accumulation phase (that is, prior to receiving payments from the annuity), his or her designated beneficiary is guaranteed to receive the amount of the original investment. In this sense, annuities look a bit like life insurance.

If the company does not offer a standard death benefit of return of principal or an enhanced death benefit for no additional cost above the standard mortality and expense (M&E) charges of 65 basis points for a no-load and 140 basis points for a commission product, hang up. If the insurance company only has "enhanced death benefit options" such as an annual step up or an annual percentage guarantee, be careful. The possibility of your beneficiaries benefiting from these is tiny compared to the additional cost you will incur. These benefits could cost you as much as an additional 30 basis points per year over a standard death benefit. I look for step-up benefits every five or six years as a nice middle ground. The likelihood of taking advantage of these are just as slim, but the cost is negligible.

SURRENDER CHARGE PERIOD

Question: Do you charge a penalty for early withdrawals? How much and for how long?

A surrender charge is usually applied to those investors who pull their money out of a variable annuity before a certain date. Is this an important issue? You bet! If the contract charges a surrender charge, be very careful about the term and amount. You do not want to be heavily penalized for withdrawing money when you may need it most. If you currently own an annuity and a broker tells you to switch it for another one with a surrender charge, run for the hills. Look for one of two types of annuities. One is a no-load that charges an M&E in the range of 65 basis points with no surrender charges, and another would be a "level load," which charges higher M&E fees but has no surrender charges. Both of these options tie the advisor income to your investment performance. I like this common interest a lot.

ANNUAL FEES AND COMPENSATION

Question: What are your mortality and expense (M&E) and administration charges?

These two features are closely related. A product with total expenses of 1.7 percent will generally have lower broker/dealer compensation (or none at all) than one with total expenses of 2.7 percent.

If the charges for a no-load are above 65 basis points, hang up. There is no reason an insurance company needs to charge that much if it's not paying commissions to an agent. The only reason would be due to enhanced death benefit options, and I already told you how I feel about those.

If the product is a level 1 percent commission product and does not have surrender charges, then it can be okay for the M&E to be as high as 150 basis points since the fee for the advisor in this case is built into the product. This is known as c-share pricing in the mutual-fund world.

If you are simply looking for a transaction and the funds in which you plan to invest are not available outside the traditional commission products, then buy the annuity that meets your needs regardless of the commission.

At this point, the features start to develop into a matrix of choices that can, at best, only be optimized when selecting which variable annuities to sell. For example, if a higher-cost annuity consistently demonstrates better performance than one with slightly lower costs, you might decide that the higher-cost variable annuity is better for you. But if the lower-cost product has more effective product features to help better address your needs, you might choose it despite inferior past performance. Remember, the past is the past. I cannot guarantee anyone where they will end up at the end of the year, but I sure can tell them where they will start. If one annuity's total cost is 150 basis points and another's is 250, you need to earn an additional 100 basis points of investment return to make up the difference. Good luck predicting that; you may want to dust off that crystal ball.

Table 19.1 presents a sample matrix of hypothetical variable annuities. Obviously, Products A, B, and C represent points on a hypothetical continuum of all variable annuity products. In summary, once you have answered the questions in this chapter and created your own matrix, you and your advisor can more easily determine the most appropriate products for you. In this example, I would go with Product A.

Lastly, since I continually preach lowering the cost that you pay the insurance company, I have included a chart of the no-load variable annuities currently on the market (Table 19.2). Remember, these are not the only ones you should review. I also believe that there are annuities that include an advisor fee that can be very attractive as well.

TABLE 19.1

Rating of Hypothetical Variable Annuities

	Product A	Product B	Product C
Insurance Co. Rating S&P	AAA	AA–	AA
No. of Variable Portfolios and Different Money Managers	25 portfolios, 4 money managers	10 portfolios, 1 money manager	25 portfolios, 10 managers
No. of Asset Classes	8	6	8
Total Annual Insurance Fees	.65%	1.40%	1.65%
Surrender Charge Period	0 years	7 years	7 years
Death Benefit	Higher of 6-year step-up, or market value	Higher of annual step-up, or market value	6% compounded
Portfolio Performance	Good	Good	Good
Broker/Dealer Compensation	0%	5.0% plus .25%	6.0% plue .20%

TABLE 19.2

No-Load Variable Annuities
Total Insurance Expense ≤ .85%

Product Name	Sub-Accounts	Insurance Expense	Portfolio Fees	Insurance Company	Phone Number
Dimensional Variable Annuity	7	0.65%	.40%–0.99%	Providian Life & Health	800-797-9177
Galaxy	4	0.55%	.70%–1.40%	American Skandia	800-541-3087
The Advisor's Edge	17	0.65%	.40%–1.50%	Providian Life & Health	800-797-9177
Scudder Horizon	6	0.70%	.50%–1.08%	Charter National	800-242-4402
T. Rowe Price	5	0.55%	.70%–1.05%	Security Benefit	800-469-6587
Touchstone	7	0.80%	.50%–1.25%	Touchstone	800-669-2796
JW Value Advantage Plus	21	0.45%	.80%–1.47%	Fortis	800-827-5877
The Schwab Variable Annuity	21	0.85%	.35%–1.75%	Great West Life	800-838-0650
Vanguard VAP	9	0.38%	.22%–0.49%	Providian Life & Health	800-523-9954

CHAPTER 20

How to Read
a Prospectus

Don't just stuff that prospectus in a desk drawer. This chapter will help you read and use it. A prospectus should be a handy reference guide for would-be variable annuity product investors. But if you don't know beforehand what to look for, reading a prospectus can be a long, tedious, confusing, and incomprehensible process.

The SEC has different checklists and forms for different types of companies that cover almost every conceivable datum about the company in question. Every prospectus must satisfy the relevant checklist requirements and forms. The problem is that the checklists and forms are revised from time to time, but the revisions don't eliminate the obsolete requirements. So, the tangled mass of requirements and legalese grows thicker with each revision. The average prospectus now contains about 50 pages of fine print. This may cause the potential investor to miss seeing the "forest" (the company) for the "trees" (all the dense, fine print of the prospectus).

I hope that in the near future, the typical prospectus will be shortened to about 10 pages of plain, readable English. As things are now, it takes a lawyer to make sense of the average prospectus, and for all we know, even your local attorney may not really understand it.

The SEC rarely makes field investigations of a company to verify the truth of the information supplied. That's why the following disclaimer appears on the cover of every SEC prospectus:

"THESE SECURITIES HAVE NOT BEEN APPROVED OR DISAPPROVED BY THE SECURITIES AND EXCHANGE COMMISSION NOR HAS THE COMMISSION PASSED UPON THE ACCURACY OF THIS PROSPECTUS. ANY REPRESENTATION TO THE CONTRARY IS A CRIMINAL OFFENSE."

This intimidating caption has been known to scare potential variable annuity customers away from some of the most conservative, safe, and established offerings. You should read it, if only for the unaccustomed joy of reading something written in plain English on a prospectus, but don't let it scare you.

There may be other disclaimers and warnings on the first few pages of a prospectus. Don't let these scare you off either. Read them, but keep in mind that they are there at the behest of lawyers and are, for the most part, just a boilerplate to get approval by the SEC. They do not contain the information you need to make a sensible judgment of an offering's merits. That's in the text of the prospectus itself.

Let's move into that dense forest of text. Here's what you want to look for:

1. **Management experience.** Look in the table of contents inside the cover to find the location referencing management experience. Have the people managing the company been doing this a long time, or are they newcomers to the business in question? Don't hesitate to ask for references!

2. **Track record.** This, too, can be found in the table of contents. The SEC requires that only the most recent three years of company history be shown here. What about the last 5 or 10 years? Ask for that information as well.

   But what if you're looking at a new mutual fund or sub-account that hasn't yet established a track record? Then look even more closely at the fund's objective. Ask to see it in writing. If they don't have a written business plan that makes sense, stay away. Don't always trust performance. Management's background and experience are the most important aspects of a new mutual fund or sub-account. You should pay particular attention to those.

3. A detailed explanation of the fund's investment objectives. If you want to invest in U.S. large cap stocks, make sure that is what the fund primarily invests in. You should also be aware that funds tend to shift assets between cash and stock, so be cognizant of the cash position. The larger the cash position, the less of your funds are actually invested in the stocks.

4 A detailed discussion of the portfolio's investment risks. This is important for those of you looking for risk in hopes of higher returns, or just the opposite. Make sure the investment risk associated with the portfolio matches your risk tolerance. Your advisor can also provide you with this information from Morningstar, a service that lists fund information and also rates them on past performance.

5. A description of the investment policies. Examples include the types of securities that may be purchased, how the fund's asset allocation may be changed, and the degree (if any) to which the manager might use options and futures.

6 An explanation of how to purchase and redeem shares. If you are a do-it-yourselfer, this will be important. If you work with an advisor, just ask him or her.

7. Shareholder transaction costs and ongoing expenses. This is a critical section usually found near the beginning of the prospectus. One of the factors that should be most important to you in the purchase of the sub-accounts is the cost associated with them. Review these and make sure that they are under 1.5 percent. If you are investing in U.S. Equities, I would not spend more than 1 percent.

8. Information on the fund's advisor. The name of the fund is irrelevant in most situations. What is important is just who the fund's advisor and subadvisor are. If they are different, pay close attention to the subadvisor. This person is actually managing the fund in most situations.

9. Names and addresses of the fund's custodian, transfer agent, and dividend-disbursing agent.

10. Telephone exchange privileges, automatic share purchase
    plans, withdrawal plans, and tax-sheltered retirement
    programs. It is always good to know your options. You
    should look in the middle of the prospectus for this type
    of data.

Prospectuses can be overwhelming, but I do recommend reading them thoroughly before investing. I am amazed at how few
people actually understand what they own.

Your next step after reviewing the prospectus is to select the
best portfolio within a given category. If you need help in the
selection of a portfolio, your advisor can step in and offer advice.

CHAPTER 21

Who Best to Purchase an Annuity From

"Seek first to understand, then to be understood."
Steven R. Covey

Variable annuities are complex investment vehicles. Investors may lack the skills necessary to make initial and continuing asset allocation decisions and to monitor performance, so an advisor may be required.

You must look carefully, however, at the motives of people giving advice. You are going to pay for that advice, either directly by paying a fee to a seasoned professional, or indirectly in bad performance and the consequences of following bad advice. Be aware of hidden motives. A situation that's good for the advisor or another investor might not be good for you. Your needs, wants, fears, and concerns—your particular situation—is unique.

A good advisor, however, can help you determine your investment needs, match the correct investment plan to your unique situation, assist you in reviewing results, and answer your questions with expertise. An advisor must get involved with your portfolio on an ongoing basis: Investing is a process, not a one-time event. Your advisor will be there when additional monies free up, or if you need to liquidate assets. Your whole financial situation can change; you'll have decisions to make that will impact previous decisions. If the economic environment shifts or there are important

personal changes in your life—a death, a birth, college—you will
have someone available who knows you and your financial picture.

CRITERIA FOR SELECTING AN INVESTMENT ADVISOR

The criteria for selecting an investment advisor include knowledge,
experience, trust, reputation—and a referral is always helpful. However, when selecting an investment advisor, you should consider one
additional feature: his or her understanding of variable annuities,
which includes a working knowledge of asset allocation and risk
management. Other considerations are the advisor's approach to
service and to monitoring the post-purchase performance.

Considering the no-load variable annuities, an investment advisor can be hired to help in the asset allocation decision and purchase of the variable annuity. Advisors, including professionals
such as attorneys, CPAs, and registered representatives, are compensated for giving advice. They can be paid for their time, as in
the case of purchasing a no-load variable annuity by fee only, or
they can be compensated by the insurance company for selling a
load variable annuity.

An investment advisor matches an investor with a variable
annuity mutual fund by first establishing the client's realistic, long-
term investment objectives with the following considerations: an
investor's return expectations, the amount of assets to be placed
under management, risk tolerance, income/cashflow needs, appropriate asset allocation, and time horizons.

DESIGNING A DETAILED ROAD MAP

The advisor helps the investor complete a detailed questionnaire
covering topics such as income needs, time horizon, risk tolerances,
general economic situation, and financial goals. The questionnaire
is different for trustees of pension or profit-sharing plans, but both
types of questionnaires are designed to find out what a particular
investor's preferences are and how that person feels his or her assets
should be managed.

The information obtained from the questionnaire is then used
to write an investment policy statement based on the investor's
return expectation and the amount of risk he or she is willing to

accept. This investment policy statement is then used to help determine appropriate investment manager candidates. Rather than selecting a variable annuity manager who favors the latest fad or the
best return in the last quarter, an investment advisor selects managers who use a discipline or style that is best suited to meeting the
objectives established in your investment policy statement.

This policy statement also serves as a written job description
for the investment manager. It is unwise to hire an advisor and
give him or her carte blanche over your account without first determining and communicating your goals and objectives. The policy statement formally communicates your needs to the investment advisor.

Investment advisors generally do not directly manage a client's money. Advisors analyze a client's objectives, establish appropriate asset allocations, introduce the client to suitable money managers, monitor their client's account, and evaluate the managers on
an ongoing basis. Some advisors do attempt to manage accounts on
their own. But since their primary job is to raise assets, how can
they also manage the accounts on a daily basis? Ask yourself that
question.

WHY NOT BUY DIRECTLY FROM THE VARIABLE ANNUITY COMPANY?

The record of any mutual fund inside a variable annuity is only as
good as those who manage it. It is not uncommon for a fund
manager to leave or change funds without informing the consumer
who is considering purchasing the fund. Shareholders are informed
but often the outsiders are not. If you do not have an advisor
looking out for these occurrences and informing you, it is possible
you would buy an annuity based on your selection of a manager
who is no longer there.

In addition, sub-account managers are concerned with how
their results relate to other sub-accounts; they can personally justify
being down 15 percent by comparing the loss to other funds that
did much worse. It is much more difficult, however, for an investment advisor to explain to you (or to an investment committee) that
after having paid an annual fee, you should be pleased with losing
only 15 percent of your capital because other investors out there
lost much more. Managers of individual accounts are more likely

to preserve client capital in down trends than are commingled sub-account managers.

Most of all, an advisor adds discipline to the process and is likely to help you ride out waves of volatility. I believe the decision to buy an annuity is a difficult one and suitability can be better determined by an advisor.

In review, the advisor insures a proper fit by following a structured process. The consulting process consists of the following six steps:

1. Analyzing your goals and objectives
2. Formulating a written investment policy document
3. Establishing appropriate asset allocations
4. Introducing suitable managers
5. Monitoring your portfolio's performance
6. Evaluating the manager on an ongoing basis

RELYING ON THE MEDIA

Most investors have little time to spend on investment monitoring, so they make investment choices based on what is promoted in the financial press or sent to them by salespeople offering investment products. Unfortunately, those wonderful advertised returns don't tell you how much risk the variable annuity sub-account managers took over a specific period of time—as we will see in the following case of Mr. and Mrs. Jones.

Barbara and Walter Jones are a retired couple. They decided to invest their lump-sum distributions of $100,000 each from their retirement funds with different variable annuity companies that they had read about in a nationally known magazine. After five years, each of their sub-accounts had grown to $201,000. In effect, they had both doubled their money.

A look behind the advertised returns of the managers reveals important risk-related information. Comparing the figures in Table 21.1 year by year reveals certain important information about each investment return.

Why was Barbara pleased and Walter upset about the results in the fifth year? The variable annuity that Walter invested with (A) increased his money almost three-fold over the first four years, yet

TABLE 21.1

Value of $100,000 with 15 Percent Annualized Return

| | Walter's Sub-Account A | | Barbara's Sub-Account B | |
Year	Gain/Loss	Portfolio Value	Gain/Loss	Portfolio Value
1	+34%	$134,000	+26%	$126,000
2	+27%	$170,000	+18%	$149,000
3	+19%	$203,000	+14%	$170,000
4	+42%	$288,000	+26%	$214,000
5	–30%	$201,000	–6%	$201,000

lost nearly one-third of its value in the fifth year. Volatility is ago-nizing for most investors.

Had Walter invested with variable annuity sub-account A at the end of their fourth year, he would have lost a significant portion of his capital.

The sub-account (B) of the variable annuity Barbara invested with took less risk to achieve the same rate of return as her hus-band's. Barbara was spared the acute anxiety that Walter went through in the fifth year.

Sub-account B was more conservative, had more consistent returns, and preserved capital more carefully. So how can you avoid what Walter went through? How do you find out how much risk a mutual fund takes? How do you get reliable information on the top sub-accounts inside the variable annuity?

Here is where the help of an investment advisor can guide you through difficult waters. An investment advisor resembles a mar-riage broker, helping you seek an investment that will be the right match for you. The media talks hype and will generally point you to the "hot fund" of the day. Investment advisors are narrow in focus, with no interest in selling insurance products, individual stocks, or other financial products. They screen fund managers across the country and across investment disciplines in order to recommend investment solutions that will match the client's finan-cial goals. They not only monitor managers and their disciplines on an ongoing basis, they also help you verify the amount of risk the manager is taking and will notify you when inside changes occur. This keeps you more aware and allows you to make decisions based on accurate information, not advertised information.

HOW DOES AN ADVISOR RECOMMEND A VARIABLE ANNUITY?

Your advisor should be knowledgeable enough to discuss with you such topics as standard deviation, Sharpe ratio, tracking error, alpha, beta, and of course in the spring, batting averages ... just checking to see if your were paying attention. These are a few measures against which advisors evaluate managers. Most advisors will recommend a variable annuity with the best diversification options for your risk tolerance at the lowest cost.

HOW TO FIND A FINANCIAL ADVISOR

Referral is one of the top ways to find a financial advisor. An individual refers you to an advisor he or she trusts. There are, however, things that you as an investor should know about your advisor. Aside from the advisor displaying honesty, integrity, experience, and product knowledge, you want somebody who has a grasp of your personal investment goals and concerns. A financial planner who understands annuities is a good place to start. (Since annuities are highly specialized and sometimes complex, some advisors do not fully understand variable annuities.)

It's fairly common for investors to interview several financial advisors before making a choice. When selecting an investment advisor, there are a number of questions that you should ask, outlined in the next section. It's important that you feel comfortable before making any commitments. You don't get a second chance at your investment program.

QUESTIONS TO ASK YOUR ADVISOR

Does the Advisor's Firm Have Any Affiliation with the Issuing Product?

It is important that you know all of the financial industry activities or affiliations your investment advisor's firm has. This will help you to determine whether your advisor may face any potential conflicts of interest, as well as the firm's level of commitment to the services you desire.

Does the advisor work for a third party? That may be okay, but an advisor who works for a third-party firm that owns a mutual fund family may be biased toward pushing one product over others. The point is to find out who you're dealing with.

Typically, an investment advisor will fall into one of the following four categories: (1) a representative of a consulting group or department affiliated with a brokerage firm, (2) a representative of an independent firm with a broker affiliate, (3) a representative of an insurance company subsidiary, (4) a non-broker/dealer-affiliated individual who offers advice and asset management but does not sell products.

You should be aware of the relationship the investment advisor has to the money management organization recommended by the advisor. Even though the association may be entirely appropriate, you should be aware of all the ways your investment advisor and his or her firm are paid by you, the investor, and/or by money management firms being recommended by the advisor.

What References Does the Advisor Have?

You should ask your investment advisor for references from clients whose situations and objectives are similar to your own. Ask your advisor how long most of his clients have been with him. If at all possible, try to get references from clients who have worked with the advisor for at least three to five years. Try to find out from the the state insurance department or the SEC if the advisor has received any customer complaints or violations. Your advisor should also be willing to furnish references from other professional organizations.

What Size Accounts Does the Advisor Handle?

Some investment advisors focus primarily on servicing large, institutional investors—such as pension funds—that have $50 million or more in assets. Others specialize in "high net worth" individuals, foundations/endowments, and small- or medium-sized pension plans ($100,000 to $50 million). Make sure you meet the minimum of the advisor before spending too much time with him or her.

What Services Does Your Advisor Provide?

There are discount brokerages and full-service brokerages. A discount brokerage will execute trades for you for a minimal fee but won't give investment advice. A full-service brokerage firm will give you advice on stocks and bonds—which ones to buy and which ones to sell—mutual funds, the whole works. Almost every so-called full-service program can provide stock and bond trading for you, but not all recommend individual securities. What's really critical is getting advice on the overall picture and deciding the best way to buy by consulting with a professional who follows the market all day, every day.

Advisors will differ in the range of services they provide, and some advisors specialize. Their expertise is in structuring a customer's investment portfolio. For investors who know their financial objectives and have a clear idea of their current financial position, the specialized expertise of an advisor may best suit their needs.

For customers who want more general help with financial strategies for coping with inflation, monthly budgeting, minimizing taxes, saving for college tuition or retirement, and estate planning, an advisor who specializes in financial planning may be more appropriate. A financial planner can also assist those who are confused about their financial situation by helping them determine where they want to be and what paths are available to achieve their goals.

How Will Your Advisor Help You with Your Investments?

Your advisor should help you establish realistic, long-term investment objectives. In doing so, your advisor should consider your expected return, how much money you're willing to risk, and if you're going to need your funds soon for a major expenditure such as buying a house or paying for a college education. Ask each advisor you interview to describe in detail how he or she determines a customer's investment objectives.

Consider whether the procedure your advisor proposes sounds logical, thorough, and effective. Ask how the plan will be customized to your situation.

The advisor you select should know how to calculate your net worth, analyze your cashflow, and prepare written plans for accumulating assets. He or she should also be able to help you coordinate any specialized help you may need from an accountant, insurance agent, or lawyer. A good advisor will also determine how much risk a customer will accept without abandoning an investment. You should ask each advisor you interview how he or she will match your investment objectives with financial opportunities.

What Is Your Advisor's Philosophy on Money Management?

Make sure your advisor's investment philosophy is consistent with your objectives. Ask each advisor you talk with what his or her particular investment biases are. Are most of the advisor's clients in junk bonds or blue-chip stocks? How long does the advisor generally suggest that clients hold their investments?

Determine whether or not your advisor consistently follows a particular strategy or style. A good money manager should have a clearly defined strategy and stick with that game plan—through good times and bad.

The variety of investment strategies a money manager may adopt seems almost limitless. Strategies go in and out of vogue. Rather than selecting an advisor who favors the latest fad, pick one who uses an approach that seems sensible to you, a strategy both you and your manager will be comfortable with given your personal objectives.

What Monitoring and Review Procedures Does the Advisor Use?

Your investment advisor updates, monitors, revises, and reviews progress toward achieving your investment objectives quarterly. Depending on your needs and situation, follow-up sessions may be scheduled monthly, quarterly, or annually. Ask your prospective investment advisors how frequently they will meet with you to review your portfolio, as well as how frequently you will receive written account statements.

Regardless of how often you personally meet with your investment advisor, insist on a minimum of quarterly written reports that measure actual performance against established objectives that you have set forth in your investment policy statement. Close communication increases the "comfort level" for both you and your investment advisor.

You should also always know who is handling your account. At larger firms, one person may initiate customer relationships, while a second individual actually manages investment portfolios. In some cases, a third person maintains ongoing customer relations.

Be sure you understand how each of these aspects of your account will be handled. If there is going to be more than one person involved, try to meet all the team players before signing on with an advisor.

How Is the Advisor Compensated?

There are three major ways in which an investment advisor is compensated: fees, commissions, or a combination of the two.

Fee-Only

Fee-only advisors set fees based on a percentage of the value of assets under management or the customer's total income, or according to a set hourly rate or fixed fee, and receive no other compensation for their services.

The fees charged by advisors vary greatly, and many advisors charge different fees depending on the size of the portfolio, the investment instruments used, and other factors. In general, advisors who offer asset management charge an annual fee anywhere from 0.5 percent to 3 percent of assets under management.

Those advisors who offer financial planning usually charge on an hourly basis, with rates ranging from $75 to $300 an hour. Some of them, however, also charge a fee based on a percentage of assets under management.

Some financial advisors charge a fixed fee, also known as a flat fee, for developing an overall investment or financial plan. Depending on the complexity of the plan, fixed fees range from $200 for a small plan to as much as $5000 or more for a comprehensive plan.

In addition to providing investment advice, some advisors publish periodic newsletters, which may include such topics as market commentary, economic news, business trends, and financial planning tips. These newsletters may be free as part of the advisor's service to his customers.

Commissions

Advisors who derive their income from commissions receive part of the funds you invest in a particular product or security, regardless of investment results. In some cases, advisors may represent that you do not pay anything for a financial plan or financial advice. If the advisor does not charge a fee either for the plan or for its implementation, he or she is likely to be receiving commissions from transaction decisions made by the investment managers he or she recommends.

If your advisor's compensation is primarily or wholly determined by commissions, the potential for conflict of interest is greatly increased. You should be aware that commission-based advisors have an incentive to sell products that pay them the largest commissions.

Your financial well-being may be influenced by how your advisor's income is determined, so be sure that your advisor fully and completely discloses how he or she will be compensated before you enter into any agreement.

Combination of Fees and Commissions

Some advisors receive a large portion of their compensation from the fees described earlier, but may also receive commissions on financial products they recommend (such as annuities or mutual funds). Using a commission to offset a fee may be entirely appropriate, as long as the relationship between a mutual fund company and the advisor is fully disclosed.

Some advisors will use a combination of commission and fee products. For clients with over $100,000 to invest, they will use no-load products and charge a fee; for clients with less than that, they will use commission products.

Never work with an advisor who sells commission products and charges a management fee on top of the commission. These products are usually very expensive and are not priced for fees to be charged in addition to the mortality costs.

What Educational Background and Credentials Does the Advisor Have?

Many stockbrokers are wrongly judged by their gold rings, what they're wearing, and the kind of car they drive. One customer confided that she chose the broker who drove the most expensive car in the parking lot. Wrong! Anyone can lease a car. Ever heard the phrase "fake it till you make it"? You're looking for someone who can be trusted, is stable, and has a solid background.

Many investment advisors are members of professional associations that have standards or examinations. You should also try to determine whether the investment advisor has a proven track record. I expect an advisor to have at least an RIA (Registered Investment Advisor). I also like the CAP and CFA designations but would not require them.

How Do Your Advisors Keep Up-to-Date in Their Fields and What Information Services Do They Provide to Their Customers?

The complexity of money management demands a high level of professional competence. Your advisor should keep up to date on the latest financial trends by taking advantage of a variety of professional education resources such as seminars, workshops, professional organizations, and subscription services.

Ask your advisor what his or her primary sources of investment information are. Does the firm have any in-house research capabilities? What external research or rating services does the advisor subscribe to? What are the key ways he or she stays abreast of the market?

What Is Your Advisor's Past Investment Performance?

Results for at least five years should be compared to market indices such as the S&P 500 Stock Index and to the results of other money managers. Some of the performance measures you should look for include:

- Consistent performance compared to the plan's goals
- Investment returns that exceed the rate of inflation
- The ability to preserve a portfolio's value in down markets

The higher the risk a customer is willing to accept, the higher the potential rewards—or losses—can be. Only you can determine your own comfort level, or the degree of risk that will still allow you to get a good night's sleep.

When evaluating performance data that an advisor has assembled, be aware that your advisor may have selected only those statistics that reflect favorably on his or her record. Performance ratings by independent agencies have more credibility than those an advisor compiles personally.

Remember that performance will vary depending on the objectives of the clients. An advisor serving conservative clients focusing on capital preservation, for example, could show moderate returns and still be performing excellently with respect to the customers' goals.

While investment returns are a factor that certainly should be considered, be careful not to choose your advisor solely on the basis of returns. Remember that the numbers you see don't tell the whole story, and past performance is no guarantee of future results.

CONCLUSION

As you can see, selecting a financial advisor is not something to be done quickly or taken lightly. There is a great deal of information to obtain, and you must evaluate an advisor's record and background very carefully. You will be entrusting this person with a very important part of your well-being: your financial health. By investing your time before you invest your money, you will be better able to select an appropriate representative.

Investing your money should never be a guessing game. By establishing a relationship with an advisor you like working with, you minimize making haphazard investment decisions. Your advisor should be your financial counselor and teacher. He or she should be dedicated to meeting your investment objectives so you can enjoy the financial rewards of investing wisely.

Most importantly, an effective investment advisor seeks first to understand, then to be understood.

CHAPTER 22

Purchasing a
Variable Annuity

There are two primary methods for purchasing a variable annuity: a lump-sum purchase and a systematic purchase. With a lump-sum purchase, an investor purchases a variable annuity with one payment. More affluent investors seeking tax-deferred wealth accumulation generally make this type of purchase. As previously discussed, lump-sum purchases are usually subject to minimum initial purchase requirements.

Many investors build wealth through systematic purchases of sub-account investment units. This method is called dollar cost averaging and is the cornerstone of many investment programs. The method dictates that the investor purchase fixed dollar amounts of variable annuity sub-accounts (units) at regular intervals, without regard to price. When prices are high, fewer units are purchased. Conversely, when prices are low, more units are purchased. The net result is that the average cost of all shares bought is lower than the average of all prices at which purchases are made. A program stressing dollar cost averaging is a long-term investment strategy. It does not guarantee that the investor will make profits. Volatility, however, is potentially reduced by this systematic approach to investing.

Just as relying on third-party referral is one of the best ways to find a good investment advisor, the same is true in purchasing a variable annuity. You want to look at the important features, evaluating the sub-account choices, the money manager, the mutual fund managers, surrender charges, fees or expenses, death benefits, and distribution features. Compare those features, benefits, and costs with other variable annuities before making a decision.

Some investment advisors will prepare an investment policy statement that will help in making a determination of the level of risk the investor wants to take and then match that up with the appropriate sub-accounts or investment styles the investor would be comfortable with.

You want to look for consistency in sub-accounts and for discipline and proven methods for reaching long-term investment goals. An investment advisor can help narrow your focus to the sub-accounts within the variable annuity and also help analyze and recommend the variable annuity program. While relying on an investment advisor, however, the investor should still pursue his or her own research and evaluation. This may help you ask the right questions.

When evaluating variable annuity sub-accounts, look at the various asset classes inside the sub-account and break those down further to understand what each of those assets means. Some variable annuities offer 35 or 40 sub-accounts and some offer less than 5. Most fall somewhere in between. Sub-accounts offer the flexibility needed to meet long-term objectives. In valuing sub-accounts, it is desirable to review the various asset types. Long-term investments (equities) will outperform other types of investments over the long term.

Once you have chosen the type of annuity you are going to buy and have your investment advisor of choice hired, you are ready to buy the annuity. The annuity purchase will include several standard forms. These forms or applications outline the structure you would like implemented for your annuity purchase. Reading and understanding these forms can be difficult, so consult your advisor.

CHAPTER 23

Getting Started

It's time to act. By now, you should have a pretty good understanding of variable annuities, investments inside sub-accounts, and what to look for in a variable annuity company.

STEP 1: CHART YOUR PERSONAL PLAN

Read this book again. Refer to it. Study the principles and follow the suggestions. Determine your financial and personal needs and time frames. Then ask for investment recommendations from the professionals you are considering, and compare these against what you have learned in this book. Do the recommendations fit your own personal financial needs?

The most important element of an investment plan is matching an investment program to your own personality and implementing a clear plan. Define all aspects of your financial needs in writing. Writing distills and clarifies your thoughts and helps break them down into workable parts.

STEP 2: ESTABLISH TIME HORIZONS

Set time horizons that match a particular investment to the eventual use of the money. If money needs to be available in less than two years, use bank certificates of deposit, savings accounts, and money market accounts. Don't use a variable annuity.

For 3- to 10-year time horizons, use mutual funds. For time horizons over 10 years use a variable annuity. A variable annuity should only be considered for a long-term horizon because (1) fees are higher, (2) taxation can be higher, and (3) the stock market goes down one year in every four, and no one has ever been able to consistently predict accurately which year it will decline. If you have short-term money in stocks and you need to withdraw it during a down year, you may take a loss.

If possible, lengthen your time horizons for investments. Every investor has expectations of having immediate performance, but those expectations may not be compatible with a particular investment style.

STEP 3: START SLOW, BUT START

With your plan completed and time horizons determined, take one or two components of your plan and start investing. Build on your plan as time goes on and you feel more confident.

STEP 4: DETERMINE THE AMOUNT OF RISK YOU CAN TAKE

It's important to determine the level of risk with which you are comfortable. For example, a 3 percent loss might be tolerable, while the possibility of a 12 percent decline in a single year might be too aggressive for you. Don't set yourself up for failure—or an ulcer.

Recognize that there are going to be down years in all investments, except fixed annuities, and you need to be ready to ride through those years. You must accept some degree of risk or you will never stay ahead of inflation and achieve financial security. It's a matter of trying to decide in advance of investing just how much risk you can handle.

STEP 5: SET REALISTIC TARGETS

Set realistic targets and match your expectations with the appropriate investments. Ask to see different mixes of investment products that have the highest probability of meeting your target rates of return, and the various amounts needed to invest to achieve those rates. Comparing different mixes will help you anchor your expectations in reality.

STEP 6: DIVERSIFY

Investing in a wide range of investments that tend to move in very different cycles lowers risk. The theory is simple: If one asset class goes down, another asset class goes up. By varying the ratio of investments in the different asset classes, an advisor can gauge the degree of risk assumed.

STEP 7: INVEST REGULARLY

Make a commitment to invest regularly. This simple strategy is one of the best and safest. Let's take a look at a 10-year investment. If you had invested $2500 in a mutual fund on June 30, 1987, and averaged a 10 percent annual return, your investment would have been worth $6484 on June 30, 1997. If you had begun adding just $50 a month on top of the $2500, and continued this monthly investment for the same 10 years, your ending balance, at the same 10 percent, would now be worth more than $16,500. A monthly investment of $100 would have increased your account to $26,630.

STEP 8: DON'T PANIC

Don't panic and sell if AUV prices inside your variable annuity go down. In fact, it's wise to expect fluctuations and ride them out. Use a drop in the market as an opportunity to average your cost downward. If you buy good variable annuity sub-accounts and compound your earnings, drops in the stock market value of the stocks will only be temporary and your patience will pay off big.

STEP 9: COPY THE INVESTMENT MASTERS

Read true accounts of successful investors, not get-rich-quick books. An excellent book is *The Prudent Investor's Guide to Beating the Market*, by John Bowen. Talk to successful people you know and ask questions. You will be surprised how open truly successful people often are.

STEP 10: HIRE A FINANCIAL ADVISOR TO GUIDE YOU AND TO PROVIDE DISCIPLINE

Choose a financial advisor you feel confident about and with whom you can communicate. Don't settle for the first person you come across. Look around, ask questions. Your advisor should clearly put your needs first and treat your money and you with consideration and respect.

Invest using professional management, another benefit of variable annuity investing. Most people need some help with their investment decisions since they don't have the time or expertise to do it all alone.

Congratulations, you've done it! You've made it through the most important parts of the book and, I hope, have started to understand the need for a variable annuity investment program. You should feel that investment success is possible due to the knowledge you've acquired. I hope I have provided the information you've been looking for to make informed choices and that you feel confident about obtaining the financial services you need to meet major life goals. If you have not purchased an annuity, look into it. If you have one, decrease your cost, increase diversification, and look for a financial advisor who has your best interests in mind.

A List of Variable Annuity Providers

Company	Variable Annuity Products	Telephone*
AAL Capital Management	AAL Variable Annuity	800-553-6319
Aetna Life Ins. & Annuity Co.	Aetna Marathon Plus Growth Plus Multi Vest Plan Variable Annuity Account C Variable Annuity Account D3	800-367-7732
Aegon Financial Services Group— PL & H	Advisor's Edge Dimensional Marquee	800-797-9177
AIG Life Insurance Co.	AIG Life Insurance Variable Acct I Alliance Gallery I Variable Annuity II	800-862-3984
Alexander Hamilton Life	Allegiance Variable Annuity	800-289-1776
Allianz Life Insurance Co.	Franklin Valuemark II	800-342-3863
Allmerica Financial Life	Allmerica Select Resource Allmerica Medallion Execannuity Plus Separate Account (A,B,C,G,H)	800-669-7353
American Enterprise Life	AE Personal Portfolio	800-333-3437
American General Life	Separate Account D Variety Plus	800-247-6584
American International Life	Variable Account A	800-362-7500
American Life Insurance Co. of NY	American Separate Account No. 2	800-872-5963
American Partners Life Insurance	Privileged Assets Select Annuity	800-297-8800
American Republic Insurance Co.	Paine Webber Advantage Annuity	800-367-6058
American Skandia Life Assurance	Advisors Choice Advisor Design Advisors Plan Alliance Capital Navigator Galaxy Variable Annuity The Lifevest Select Stagecoach	800-704-6201

* *Note:* Phone numbers are accurate as of 1997.

Company	Variable Annuity Products	Telephone*
American United Life Insurance	AUL American Unit Trust	800-634-1629
Ameritas Variable Life Ins.	Overture Annuity II Overture Annuity III Plus	800-634-8353
Anchor National Life Insurance	American Pathway II ICAP II Polaris	800-445-7861
Annuity Investors Life Ins.	Commodore Mariner Commodore Nauticus VA Commodore Americus	800-789-6771
Canada Life Ins. of America	Trillium Varifund Annuity	800-905-1959
Charter National Life	Scudder Horizon Plan	800-225-2470
CNA	Capital Select Variable Annuity Capital Select Equity Index Annuity	800-262-1755
Conn. General Life Ins. CIGNA	CIGNA ACCRU Variable Annuity	800-628-2811
COVA Financial Services Life	COVA Variable Annuity	800-343-8496
Dreyfus	Dreyfus/Transamerica Triple Advantage	800-258-4260
Equitable Life Assurance Soc.	Accumulator Equi-Vest Equi-Vest Personal Ret Program Income Manager Accumulator Income Manager Rollover Momentum Momentum Plus Rollover IRA	800-628-6673
Equitable Life of Iowa	Equi-Select	800-344-6864
The Hartford	The Director The Director I Dean Witter Select Dimensions	800-862-6668
IDS	Flexible Portfolio Annuity IDS Life Flexible Annuity Symphony	800-437-0602
Farm Bureau Life Ins. Co.	Farm Bureau Life VA	800-247-4170
Fidelity Inv. Life Ins. Co.	Fidelity Retirement Reserves	800-544-2442

Company	Variable Annuity Products	Telephone*
Fidelity Standard Life	Fidelity Standard Life Separate Acct	800-283-4536
First Investors Life Ins.	Execannuity Plus (NY)	800-832-7783
1st Providian Life & Health	Vanguard Variable Annuity Plan (NY)	800-523-9954
First SunAmerican Life	First SunAmerica ICAP II (NY) First SunAmerica Polaris	800-996-9786
First Transamerica Life	Dryfus/Transamerica Triple Advantage	800-258-4260
First Variable Life Ins. Co.	Vista Annuity/Capital Five VA Capital No Load Annuity	800-228-1035
Fortis Benefits Ins. Co.	Fortis Masters VA Fortis Opportunity VA Fortis Value Advantage Plus VA Fortis Benefits Ins. Co.	800-800-2638
General American Life	G.T. Global Allocator General American Step Acct. Two	800-233-6699
Glenbrook Life & Annuity	AIM Lifetime Plus VA STI Classic VA	800-776-6978
Golden American Life Ins.	Fund For Life Golden Select (2D) Golden Select DVA Plus	800-243-3706
Great American RSV Insurance	Great American RSV VA Acct C Great American RSV VAE	317-571-3700
Great Northern Ins. Annuity Corp.	Paragon Power Portfolio VA	800-455-0870
Great West Life & Annuity	Future Funds Series Account Maximum Value Plan (MVP)	800-468-8661
Guardian Ins. & Annuity	Guardian Investor Value Guard II	800-221-3253
Integrity Life Insurance Co. ARM Financiall Group	Grandmaster II Pinnacle OMNI New Momentum	800-325-8583
John Hancock	Accumulator Accommodator 2000 Independence Independence Preferred Declaration	800-732-5543

Company	Variable Annuity Products	Telephone*
Jackson National Life	JNL Perspective	800-873-5654
Jefferson-Pilot Life	Alpha Alpha Flex Jefferson-Pilot Separate Acct A	910-691-3448
Kemper Investors	Kemper Advantage III Kemper Passport	800-554-5426
Keyport Life Insurance	Keyport Preferred Advisor Preferred Advisor	800-367-3654
Life Insurance Co. of Virginia	Commonwealth Variable Annuity Plus	800-352-9910
Lincoln Benefit Life	Investors Select Investors Select Variable Annuity	800-865-5237
Lincoln National Life	American Legacy American Legacy II American Funds	800-443-8137
Lutheran Brotherhood	LB VIP Variable Annuity	800-423-7056
Manufacturers Life	Lifetrust 1 Lifestyle Fixed	800-827-4546
MFS Sun Life of Canada	MFS Regatta Gold MFS Regatta Compass-3	800-752-7216
MassMutual	Flex Extra Flex Extra (2) Lifetrust Panorama Panorama Plus Panorama Premier	413-788-8411
Merrill Lynch Life Ins. Co.	Portfolio Plus Retirement Plus (A) Retirement Plus (B)	800-535-5549
MetLife	The Preference Plus Account	800-553-4459
Midland National Life	Separate Account C	800-638-5000
Minnesota Mutual Life	Megannuity Multioption Flexible Annuity	800-443-3677
MML Bay State Life Ins.	Lifetrust 1	800-272-2216
Mony Life Ins. Co. of America	Keynote The Moneymaster The Valuemaster	800-487-6669

Company	Variable Annuity Products	Telephone*
Mutual of America Life	Mutual of America Separate Acct 2	800-463-3785
National Integrity Life	Grandmaster (NI) Grandmaster II (NI) Pinnacle	800-433-1778
Nationwide	Best of Americas Vision Best of America III Best of America IV DCVA DCVA - TSA Fidelity Advisor Classic Fidelity Advisor Annuity Select MFS Spectrum Multi-Flex Nationwide Variable Account 3 NEA Valuebuilder Annuity Nationwide Life & Annuity VA (A) One Investors Annuity	888-867-5175
New York Life	Facilitator (I) Facilitator (II) Lifestages NYLIAC VA I NYLIAC VA II (Qualified)	212-576-6569
North American Security Life	Venture Venture Vision	800-334-4437
Northbrook Life Ins. Co.	Dean Witter Variable Annuity	800-654-2397
Northern Life	Northern Life Advantage	800-870-0453
Northwestern National Life	Northstar NWNL Variable Annuity Select Annuity II Select Annuity III	800-621-3750
Ohio National Life Insurance Co.	Top A (A) Top A (B) Top Plus (B)	800-366-6654
Pacific Corinthian Life	Pacific Corinthian Variable Annuity	619-452-9060
Pacific Mutual Life	Pacific Select Variable Annuity Pacific Select Variable Annuity One Pacific Portfolios	800-722-2333

Company	Variable Annuity Products	Telephone*
Paine Webber Life Insurance	Paine Webber Milestones B Paine Webber Milestones D	800-552-5622
Penn Insurance & Annuity	Pennant	800-548-1119
Penn Mutual Life Insurance	Diversifier II	800-548-1119
PFL Life Insurance	Endeavor Variable Annuity Fidelity Income Plus	800-525-6205
Phoenix Home Mutual	Big Edge Big Edge Choice Big Edge Plus Templeton Investment Plus	800-243-4361
Principal Mutual Life Insurance	Pension Builder Plus Principal Variable Annuity	800-986-3343
Protective Life Insurance Co.	Protective Variable Annuity	800-456-6330
Provident Mutual Life & Annuity	Market Street VIP Market Street VIP (2) Options VIP	610-407-1717
Providian Life & Health	Marquee Variable Annuity Providian Prism The Advisor,s Edge	800-866-6007
Pruco Insurance Co. of NJ	Discovery Select Discovery Plus (NJ)	201-802-6000
Prudential Insurance Co.	Variable Investment Plan Discovery Plus Discovery Select	800-445-4571
Putman	Capital Manager	800-225-1581
SAFECO Life Insurance Co.	Spinnaker Q & NQ Flex Spinnaker Plus Mainsail SAFECO Resource Acct A SAFECO Resource Acct B	800-426-6730
Schwab	Schwab Variable Annuity	800-838-0650
Security Benefit Life	Parkstone Variable Annuity SBL Variable Annuity Acct III SBL Variable Annuity Acct IV Variflex LS Variflex T. Rowe Price Variable Annuity	800-888-2461 800-541-8803
Security First Life Ins.	Flexible Bonus Investors Choice Strive	800-284-4536

Company	Variable Annuity Products	Telephone*
Security Life of Denver	Exchequer Variable Annuity	800-933-5858
Sun Life Assurance of Canada	MFS Regatta Gold MFS Regatta Compass 3 Compass 2	800-752-7216
TIAA	College Retirement Equities Fund	800-842-2776
Templeton	Templeton Imm. Variable Annuity	800-292-9293
Touchstone	Touchstone Variable Annuity Touchstone Variable Annuity II	800-669-2796
Transamerica Occidental Life Ins. Co.	Schwab Investment Advantage Dryfus/Transamer Triple Advantage	800-258-4260
Travelers	Universal Annuity Vintage Portfolio Architect	800-334-4298
Union Central Life Insurance	Carillon Account	800-825-1551
United Companies Life Insurance	Spectraselect	800-825-7568
United Investors Life	Advantage II	800-999-0317
United of Omaha Life Ins. Co.	Ultrannuity Series V	800-453-4933
USAA Life Insurance Co.	USAA Life Variable Annuity	800-531-6390
Vanguard (Providian Life & Health)	Vanguard Variable Annuity	800-522-5555
Variable Annuity Life Ins.	Portfolio Directory 2 Independence Plus Portfolio Director Portfolio Director 2	800-228-2542
Western Reserve Life	Janus Retirement Advantage WRL Freedom Attainer WRL Freedom Bellwether WRL Freedom Conqueror C.A.S.E Reserve Variable Annuity Meridian/INVESCO Sector VA	800-443-9974 ext. 6510

Internal Revenue Code Sections

Internal Revenue Code Section 72
Annuities, Certain Proceeds of Endowment, and
Life Insurance Contracts

GENERAL RULE FOR ANNUITIES

Except as otherwise provided in this chapter, gross income includes
any amount received as an annuity (whether for a period certain or
during one or more lives) under an annuity, endowment, or life
insurance contract.

EXCLUSION RATIO IN GENERAL

Gross income does not include that part of any amount received as
an annuity under an annuity, endowment, or life insurance contract
which bears the same ratio to such amount as the investment in the
contract (as of the annuity starting date) bears to the expected
return under the contract (as of such date).

EXCLUSION LIMITED TO INVESTMENT

The portion of any amount received as an annuity which is excluded from gross income shall not exceed the unrecovered investment in the contract immediately before the receipt of such amount.

DEDUCTION WHERE ANNUITY PAYMENTS
CEASE BEFORE ENTIRE INVESTMENT
RECOVERED IN GENERAL

If—after the annuity starting date, payments as an annuity under
the contract cease by reason of the death of an annuitant, and as of
the date of such cessation, there is unrecovered investment in the
contract, the amount of such unrecovered investment (in excess of
any amount specified in subsection (e)(5) which was not included
in gross income) shall be allowed as a deduction to the annuitant
for his last taxable year.

PAYMENTS TO OTHER PERSONS

In the case of any contract which provides for payments meeting the requirements of subparagraphs (B) and (C) of subsection (c)(2), the deduction under subparagraph (A) shall be allowed to the person entitled to such payments for the taxable year in which such payments are received.

NET OPERATING LOSS DEDUCTIONS PROVIDED

For purposes of section 172, a deduction allowed under this paragraph shall be treated as if it were attributable to a trade or business of the taxpayer.

UNRECOVERED INVESTMENT

For purposes of this subsection, the unrecovered investment in the contract as of any date is—the investment in the contract as of the annuity starting date, reduced by the aggregate amount received under the contract on or after such annuity starting date and before the date as of which the determination is being made, to the extent such amount was excludable from gross income under this subtitle.

DEFINITIONS

INVESTMENT IN THE CONTRACT

For purposes of subsection (b), the investment in the contract as of the annuity starting date is—the aggregate amount of premiums or other consideration paid for the contract, minus the aggregate amount received under the contract before such date, to the extent that such amount was excludable from gross income under this subtitle or prior income tax laws.

ADJUSTMENT IN INVESTMENT WHERE THERE IS REFUND FEATURE

If—the expected return under the contract depends in whole or in part on the life expectancy of one or more individuals; the contract provides for payments to be made to a beneficiary (or to the estate of an annuitant) on or after the death of the annuitant or annuitants; and such payments are in the nature of a refund of the consideration paid, then the value (computed without discount for interest) of such payments on the annuity starting date shall be subtracted from the amount determined under paragraph (1). Such value shall be computed in accordance with actuarial tables prescribed by the Secretary. For purposes of this paragraph and of subsection (e)(2)(A), the term "refund of the consideration paid" includes amounts payable after the death of an annuitant by reason of a provision in the contract for a life annuity with minimum period of payments certain, but if part of the consideration was contributed by an employer does not include that part of any payment to a beneficiary (or to the estate of the annuitant) which is not attributable to the consideration paid by the employee for the contract as determined under paragraph (1)(A).

EXPECTED RETURN

For purposes of subsection (b), the expected return under the contract shall be determined as follows:

LIFE EXPECTANCY

If the expected return under the contract, for the period on and after the annuity starting date, depends in whole or in part on the life expectancy of one or more individuals, the expected return shall be computed with reference to actuarial tables prescribed by the Secretary.

INSTALLMENT PAYMENTS

If subparagraph (A) does not apply, the expected return is the aggregate of the amounts receivable under the contract as an annuity.

ANNUITY STARTING DATE

For purposes of this section, the annuity starting date in the case of any contract is the first day of the first period for which an amount is received as an annuity under the contract; except that if such date was before January 1, 1954, then the annuity starting date is January 1, 1954.

TREATMENT OF EMPLOYEE CONTRIBUTIONS UNDER DEFINED CONTRIBUTION PLANS AS SEPARATE CONTRACTS

For purposes of this section, employee contributions (and any income allocable thereto) under a defined contribution plan may be treated as a separate contract.

AMOUNTS NOT RECEIVED AS ANNUITIES

APPLICATION OF SUBSECTION IN GENERAL

This subsection shall apply to any amount which—
is received under an annuity, endowment, or life insurance contract, and is not received as an annuity, if no provision of this subtitle (other than this subsection) applies with respect to such amount.

DIVIDENDS

For purposes of this section, any amount received which is in the nature of a dividend or similar distribution shall be treated as an amount not received as an annuity.

GENERAL RULE

Any amount to which this subsection applies—
if received on or after the annuity starting date, shall be included in gross income, or if received before the annuity starting date—
shall be included in gross income to the extent allocable to income on the contract, and shall not be included in gross income to the extent allocable to the investment in the contract.

ALLOCATION OF AMOUNTS TO INCOME AND INVESTMENT

For purposes of paragraph (2)(B)—

ALLOCATION TO INCOME

Any amount to which this subsection applies shall be treated as allocable to income on the contract to the extent that such amount does not exceed the excess (if any) of—the cash value of the contract (determined without regard to any surrender charge) immediately before the amount is received, over the investment in the contract at such time.

ALLOCATION TO INVESTMENT

Any amount to which this subsection applies shall be treated as allocable to investment in the contract to the extent that such amount is not allocated to income under subparagraph (A).

SPECIAL RULES FOR APPLICATION OF PARAGRAPH (2)(B)

For purposes of paragraph (2)(B)—

LOANS TREATED AS DISTRIBUTIONS

If, during any taxable year, an individual—receives (directly or indirectly) any amount as a loan under any contract to which this subsection applies, or assigns or pledges (or agrees to assign or pledge) any portion of any such contract, such amount or portion shall be treated as received under the contract as an amount not received as an annuity. The preceding sentence shall not apply for purposes of determining investment in the contract, except that the investment in the contract shall be increased by any amount included in gross income by reason of the amount treated as received under the preceding sentence.

TREATMENT OF POLICYHOLDER DIVIDENDS

Any amount described in paragraph (1)(B) shall not be included in gross income under paragraph (2)(B)(i) to the extent such amount is retained by the insurer as a premium or other consideration paid for the contract.

TREATMENT OF TRANSFERS WITHOUT ADEQUATE CONSIDERATION

In general if an individual who holds an annuity contract transfers it without full and adequate consideration, such individual shall be treated as receiving an amount equal to the excess of—the cash surrender value of such contract at the time of transfer, over the investment in such contract at such time, under the contract as an amount not received as an annuity.

EXCEPTION FOR CERTAIN TRANSFERS BETWEEN SPOUSES OR FORMER SPOUSES

Clause (i) shall not apply to any transfer to which section 1041(a) (relating to transfers of property between spouses or incident to divorce) applies.

ADJUSTMENT TO INVESTMENT IN CONTRACT OF TRANSFEREE

If under clause (i) an amount is included in the gross income of the transferer of an annuity contract, the investment in the contract of the transferee in such contract shall be increased by the amount so included.

RETENTION OF EXISTING RULES IN CERTAIN CASES IN GENERAL

In any case to which this paragraph applies—paragraphs (2)(B) and (4)(A) shall not apply, and if paragraph (2)(A) does not apply, the amount shall be included in gross income, but only to the extent it exceeds the investment in the contract.

EXISTING CONTRACTS

This paragraph shall apply to contracts entered into before August 14, 1982. Any amount allocable to investment in the contract after August 13, 1982, shall be treated as from a contract entered into after such date.

CERTAIN LIFE INSURANCE AND ENDOWMENT CONTRACTS

Except as provided in paragraph (10) and except to the extent prescribed by the Secretary by regulations, this paragraph shall apply to any amount not received as an annuity which is received under a life insurance or endowment contract.

CONTRACTS UNDER QUALIFIED PLANS

Except as provided in paragraph (8), this paragraph shall apply to any amount received—from a trust described in section 401(a) which is exempt from tax under section 501(a), from a contract— purchased by a trust described in clause (i), 403(a), purchased as part of a plan described in section 403(a), described in section 403(b), or provided for employees of a life insurance company under a plan described in section 818(a)(3), or from an individual retirement account or an individual retirement annuity. Any dividend described in section 404(k) which is received by a participant or beneficiary shall, for purposes of this subparagraph, be treated as paid under a separate contract to which clause (ii)(I) applies.

FULL REFUNDS, SURRENDERS, REDEMPTIONS, AND MATURITIES

This paragraph shall apply to—any amount received, whether in a single sum or otherwise, under a contract in full discharge of the obligation under the contract which is in the nature of a refund of the consideration paid for the contract, and any amount received under a contract on its complete surrender, redemption, or maturity. In the case of any amount to which the preceding sentence applies, the rule of paragraph (2)(A) shall not apply.

INVESTMENT IN THE CONTRACT

For purposes of this subsection, the investment in the contract as of any date is—the aggregate amount of premiums or other consideration paid for the contract before such date, minus the aggregate amount received under the contract before such date, to the extent that such amount was excludable from gross income under this subtitle or prior income tax laws. [(7) Repealed. Pub. L. 100-647, title I, 1011A(b)(9)(A), Nov. 10, 1988, 102 Stat. 3474]

EXTENSION OF PARAGRAPH (2)(B) TO QUALIFIED PLANS IN GENERAL

Notwithstanding any other provision of this subsection, in the case of any amount received before the annuity starting date from a trust or contract described in paragraph (5)(D), paragraph (2)(B) shall apply to such amounts.

ALLOCATION OF AMOUNT RECEIVED

For purposes of paragraph (2)(B), the amount allocated to the investment in the contract shall be the portion of the amount described in subparagraph (A) which bears the same ratio to such amount as the investment in the contract bears to the account balance. The determination under that preceding sentence shall be made as of the time of the distribution or at such other time as the Secretary may prescribe.

TREATMENT OF FORFEITABLE RIGHTS

If an employee does not have a nonforfeitable right to any amount under any trust or contract to which subparagraph (A) applies, such amount shall not be treated as part of the account balance.

INVESTMENT IN THE CONTRACT BEFORE 1987

In the case of a plan which on May 5, 1986, permitted withdrawal of any employee contributions before separation from service, subparagraph (A) shall apply only to the extent that amounts received before the annuity starting date (when increased by amounts previously received under the contract after December 31, 1986) exceed the investment in the contract as of December 31, 1986.

[(9) Repealed. Pub. L. 100-647, title I, 1011A(b)(2)(B), Nov. 10, 1988, 102 Stat. 3473]

TREATMENT OF MODIFIED ENDOWMENT CONTRACTS IN GENERAL

Notwithstanding paragraph (5)C, in the case of any modified endowment contract (as defined in section 7702A)—paragraphs (2)(B) and (4)(A) shall apply, and in applying paragraph (4)(A), "any person" shall be substituted for "an individual."

TREATMENT OF CERTAIN BURIAL CONTRACTS

Notwithstanding subparagraph (A), paragraph (4)(A) shall not apply in any assignment (or pledge) of a modified endowment contract if such assignment (or pledge) is solely to cover the payment of expenses referred to in section 7702(e)(2)(C)(iii) and if the maximum death benefit under such contract does not exceed $225,000.

ANTI-ABUSE RULES IN GENERAL

For purposes of determining the amount included in gross income under this subsection—all modified endowment contracts issued by the same company to the same policyholder during any calendar year shall be treated as 1 modified endowment contract, and all annuity contracts issued by the same company to the same policyholder during any calendar year shall be treated as 1 annuity contract. The preceding sentence shall not apply to any contract described in paragraph (5)(D).

REGULATORY AUTHORITY

The Secretary may by regulations prescribe such additional rules as may be necessary or appropriate to prevent avoidance of the purposes of this subsection through serial purchases of contracts or otherwise.

SPECIAL RULES FOR COMPUTING EMPLOYEES' CONTRIBUTIONS

In computing, for purposes of subsection C(1)(A), the aggregate amount of premiums or other consideration paid for the contract, and for purposes of subsection (e)(6), the aggregate premiums or other consideration paid, amounts contributed by the employer shall be included, but only to the extent that—such amounts were includible in the gross income of the employee under this subtitle or prior income tax laws, or if such amounts had been paid directly to the employee at the time they were contributed, they would not have been includible in the gross income of the employee under the law applicable at the time of such contribution.

Paragraph (2) shall not apply to amounts which were contributed by the employer after December 31, 1962, and which would not have been includible in the gross income of the employee by reason of the application of section 911 if such amounts had been paid directly to the employee at the time of contribution. The preceding sentence shall not apply to amounts which were contributed by the employer, as determined under regulations prescribed by the Secretary, to provide pension or annuity credits, to the extent such credits are attributable to services performed before January 1, 1963, and are provided pursuant to pension or annuity plan provisions in existence on March 12, 1962, and on that date applicable to such services.

RULES FOR TRANSFEREE WHERE TRANSFER WAS FOR VALUE

Where any contract (or any interest therein) is transferred (by assignment or otherwise) for a valuable consideration, to the extent that the contract (or interest therein) does not, in the hands of the transferee, have a basis which is determined by reference to the basis in the hands of the transferor, then—for purposes of this section, only the actual value of such consideration, plus the amount of the premiums and other consideration paid by the transferee after the transfer, shall be taken into account in computing the aggregate amount of the premiums or other consideration paid for the contract; for purposes of subsection C(1)(B), there shall be taken into account only the aggregate amount received under the contract by the transferee before the annuity starting date, to the extent that such amount was excludable from gross income under this subtitle or prior income tax laws; and the annuity starting date is January 1, 1954, or the first day of the first period for which the transferee received an amount under the contract as an annuity, whichever is the later.

For purposes of this subsection, the term "transferee" includes a beneficiary of, or the estate of, the transferee.

OPTION TO RECEIVE ANNUITY IN LIEU OF LUMP SUM

If—a contract provides for payment of a lump sum in full discharge of an obligation under the contract, subject to an option to receive an annuity in lieu of such lump sum; the option is exercised within 60 days after the day on which such lump sum first became payable; and part or all of such lump sum would (but for this subsection) be includible in gross income by reason of subsection (e)(1), then, for purposes of this subtitle, no part of such lump sum shall be considered as includible in gross income at the time such lump sum first became payable.

[(i) Repealed. Pub. L. 94-455, title XIX, 1951(b)(1)(A), Oct. 4, 1976, 90 Stat. 1836]

INTEREST

Notwithstanding any other provision of this section, if any amount is held under an agreement to pay interest thereon, the interest payments shall be included in gross income.

[(k) Repealed. Pub. L. 98-369, div. A, title IV, 421(b)(1), July 18, 1984, 98 Stat. 794]

FACE-AMOUNT CERTIFICATES

For purposes of this section, the term "endowment contract" includes a face-amount certificate, as defined in section 2(a)(15) of the Investment Company Act of 1940 (15 U.S.C., sec. 80a-2), issued after December 31, 1954.

SPECIAL RULES APPLICABLE TO EMPLOYEE ANNUITIES AND DISTRIBUTIONS UNDER EMPLOYEE PLANS

[(1) Repealed. Pub. L. 93-406, title II, 2001(h)(2), Sept. 2, 1974, 88 Stat. 957]

COMPUTATION OF CONSIDERATION PAID BY THE EMPLOYEE

In computing—the aggregate amount of premiums or other consideration paid for the contract for purposes of subsection (c)(1)(A) (relating to the investment in the contract), the consideration for the contract contributed by the employee for purposes of subsection (d)(1) (relating to employee's contributions recoverable in 3 years) and subsection (e)(7) (relating to plans where substantially all contributions are employee contributions), and the aggregate premiums or other consideration paid for purposes of subsection (e)(6) (relating to certain amounts not received as an annuity), any amount allowed as a deduction with respect to the contract under section 404 which was paid while the employee was an employee within the meaning of section 401C(1) shall be treated as consideration contributed by the employer, and there shall not be taken into account any portion of the premiums or other consideration for the contract paid while the employee was an owner employee which is properly allocable (as determined under regulations prescribed by the Secretary) to the cost of life, accident, health, or other insurance.

LIFE INSURANCE CONTRACTS

This paragraph shall apply to any life insurance contract—purchased as a part of a plan described in section 403(a), or purchased by a trust described in section 401(a) which is exempt from tax under section 501(a) if the proceeds of such contract are payable directly or indirectly to a participant in such trust or to a beneficiary of such participant. Any contribution to a plan described in subparagraph (A)(i) or a trust described in subparagraph (A)(ii) which is allowed as a deduction under section 404, and any income of a trust described in subparagraph (A)(ii), which is determined in accordance with regulations prescribed by the Secretary to have been applied to purchase the life insurance protection under a contract described in subparagraph (A), is includible in the gross income of the participant for the taxable year when so applied.

In the case of the death of an individual insured under a contract described in subparagraph (A), an amount equal to the cash surrender value of the contract immediately before the death of the insured shall be treated as a payment under such plan or a distribution by such trust, and the excess of the amount payable by reason of the death of the insured over such cash surrender value shall not be includible in gross income under this section and shall be treated as provided in section 101.

[(4) Repealed. Pub. L. 97-248, title II, 236(b)(1), Sept. 3, 1982, 96 Stat. 510]

PENALTIES APPLICABLE TO CERTAIN AMOUNTS RECEIVED BY 5-PERCENT OWNERS

This paragraph applies to amounts which are received from a qualified trust described in section 401(a) or under a plan described in section 403(a) at any time by an individual who is, or has been, a 5-percent owner, or by a successor of such an individual, under regulations prescribed by the Secretary, to exceed the benefits provided for such individual under the plan formula.

If a person receives an amount to which this paragraph applies, his tax under this chapter for the taxable year in which such amount is received shall be increased by an amount equal to 10 percent of the portion of the amount so received which is includible in his gross income for such taxable year.

For purposes of this paragraph, the term "5-percent owner" means any individual who, at any time during the 5 plan years preceding the plan year ending in the taxable year in which the amount is received, is a 5-percent owner (as defined in section 416(i)(1)(B)).

OWNER-EMPLOYEE DEFINED

For purposes of this subsection, the term "owner-employee" has the meaning assigned to it by section 401C(3) and includes an individual for whose benefit an individual retirement account or annuity described in section 408(a) or (b) is maintained. For purposes of the preceding sentence, the term "owner-employee" shall include an employee within the meaning of section 401(c)(1).

MEANING OF DISABLED

For purposes of this subsection, an individual shall be considered to be disabled if he is unable to engage in any substantial gainful activity by reason of any medically determinable physical or mental impairment which can be expected to result in death or to be of long-continued and indefinite duration. An individual shall not be considered to be disabled unless he furnishes proof of the existence thereof in such form and manner as the Secretary may require. [(8) Repealed. Pub. L. 97-248, title II, 236(b)(1), Sept. 3, 1982, 96 Stat. 510] [(9) Repealed. Pub. L. 98-369, div. A., title VII, 713(d)(1), July 18, 1984, 98 Stat 957]

DETERMINATION OF INVESTMENT IN THE CONTRACT IN THE CASE OF QUALIFIED DOMESTIC RELATIONS ORDERS

Under regulations prescribed by the Secretary, in the case of a distribution or payment made to an alternate payee who is the spouse or former spouse of the participant pursuant to a qualified domestic relations order (as defined in section 414(p)), the investment in the contract as of the date prescribed in such regulations shall be allocated on a pro rata basis between the present value of such distribution or payment and the present value of all other benefits payable with respect to the participant to which such order relates.

ANNUITIES UNDER RETIRED SERVICEMAN'S FAMILY PROTECTION PLAN OR SURVIVOR BENEFIT PLAN

Subsection (b) shall not apply in the case of amounts received after December 31, 1965, as an annuity under chapter 73 of title 10 of the United States Code, but all such amounts shall be excluded from gross income until there has been so excluded (under section

122(b)(1) or this section, including amounts excluded before January 1, 1966) an amount equal to the consideration for the contract (as defined by section 122(b)(2)), plus any amount treated pursuant to section 101(b)(2)(D) as additional consideration paid by the employees. Thereafter all amounts so received shall be included in gross income.

SPECIAL RULES FOR DISTRIBUTIONS FROM QUALIFIED PLANS TO WHICH EMPLOYEE MADE DEDUCTIBLE CONTRIBUTIONS

TREATMENT OF CONTRIBUTIONS

For purposes of this section and sections 402 and 403, notwithstanding section 414(h), any deductible employee contribution made to a qualified employer plan or government plan shall be treated as an amount contributed by the employer which is not includible in the gross income of the employee.

[(2) Repealed. Pub. L. 100-647, title I, 1011A(c)(8), Nov. 10, 1988, 102 Stat.. 3476]

AMOUNTS CONSTRUCTIVELY RECEIVED
IN GENERAL

For purposes of this subsection, rules similar to the rules provided by subsection (p) (other than the exception contained in paragraph (2) thereof) shall apply.

PURCHASE OF LIFE INSURANCE

To the extent any amount of accumulated deductible employee contributions of an employee are applied to the purchase of life insurance contracts, such amount shall be treated as distributed to the employee in the year so applied.

SPECIAL RULE FOR TREATMENT OF
ROLLOVER AMOUNTS

For purposes of sections 402C, 403(a)(4), and 408(d)(3), the Secretary shall prescribe regulations providing for such allocations of amounts attributable to accumulated deductible employee contributions, and for such other rules, as may be necessary to insure that such accumulated deductible employee contributions do not become eligible for additional tax benefits (or freed from limitations) through the use of rollovers.

DEFINITIONS AND SPECIAL RULES

For purposes of this subsection—

DEDUCTIBLE EMPLOYEE CONTRIBUTIONS

The term "deductible employee contributions" means any qualified voluntary employee contribution (as defined in section 219(e)(2)) made after December 31, 1981, in a taxable year beginning after such date and made for a taxable year beginning before January 1, 1987, and allowable as a deduction under section 219(a) for such taxable year.

ACCUMULATED DEDUCTIBLE EMPLOYEE CONTRIBUTIONS

The term "accumulated deductible employee contributions" means the deductible employee contributions—increased by the amount of income and gain allocable to such contributions, and reduced by the sum of the amount of loss and expense allocable to such contributions and the amounts distributed with respect to the employee which are attributable to such contributions (or income or gain allocable to such contributions).

QUALIFIED EMPLOYER PLAN

The term "qualified employer plan" has the meaning given to such term by subsection (p)(3)(A)(I).

GOVERNMENT PLAN

The term "government plan" has the meaning given such term by subsection (p)(3)(B).

ORDERING RULES

Unless the plan specifies otherwise, any distribution from such plan shall not be treated as being made from the accumulated deductible employee contributions, until all other amounts to the credit of the employee have been distributed.

LOANS TREATED AS DISTRIBUTIONS

For purposes of this section—

TREATMENT AS DISTRIBUTIONS

LOANS

If during any taxable year a participant or beneficiary receives (directly or indirectly) any amount as a loan from a qualified employer plan, such amount shall be treated as having been received by such individual as a distribution under such plan.

ASSIGNMENTS OR PLEDGES

If during any taxable year a participant or beneficiary assigns (or agrees to assign) or pledges (or agrees to pledge) any portion of his interest in a qualified employer plan, such portion shall be treated as having been received by such individual as a loan from such plan.

EXCEPTION FOR CERTAIN LOANS

GENERAL RULE

Paragraph (1) shall not apply to any loan to the extent that such loan (when added to the outstanding balance of all other loans from such plan whether made on, before, or after August 13, 1982), does not exceed the lesser of—$50,000, reduced by the excess (if any) of—the highest outstanding balance of loans from the plan during the 1-year period ending on the day before the date on which such loan was made, over the outstanding balance of loans from the plan on the date on which such loan was made, or the greater of (I) one-half of the present value of the nonforfeitable accrued benefit of the employee under the plan, or (II) $10,000. For purposes of clause (ii), the present value of the nonforfeitable accrued benefit shall be determined without regard to any accumulated deductible employee contributions (as defined in subsection (o)(5)(B)).

REQUIREMENT THAT LOAN BE REPAYABLE WITHIN 5 YEARS IN GENERAL

Subparagraph (A) shall not apply to any loan unless such loan, by its terms, is required to be repaid within 5 years.

EXCEPTION FOR HOME LOANS

Clause (i) shall not apply to any loan used to acquire any dwelling unit which within a reasonable time is to be used (determined at the time the loan is made) as the principal residence of the participant.

REQUIREMENT OF LEVEL AMORTIZATION

Except as provided in regulations, this paragraph shall not apply to any loan unless substantially level amortization of such loan (with payments not less frequently than quarterly) is required over the term of the loan.

RELATED EMPLOYERS AND RELATED PLANS

For purposes of this paragraph—the rules of subsection (b), (c), and (m) of section 414 shall apply, and all plans of an employer (determined after the application of such subsections) shall be treated as 1 plan.

DENIAL OF INTEREST DEDUCTIONS IN CERTAIN CASES

IN GENERAL

No deduction otherwise allowable under this chapter shall be allowed under this chapter for any interest paid or accrued on any loan to which paragraph (1) does not apply by reason of paragraph (2) during the period described in subparagraph (B).

PERIOD TO WHICH SUBPARAGRAPH (A) APPLIES

For purposes of subparagraph (A), the period described in this subparagraph is the period—on or after the 1st day on which the individual to whom the loan is made is a key employee (as defined in section 416(i)), or such loan is secured by amounts attributable to elective deferrals described in subparagraph (A) or (C) of section 402(g)(3).

QUALIFIED EMPLOYER PLAN, ETC.

For purposes of this subsection—

QUALIFIED EMPLOYER PLAN

In general, the term "qualified employer plan" means—a plan described in section 401(a) which includes a trust exempt from tax under section 501(a), an annuity plan described in section 403(a), and a plan under which amounts are contributed by an individual's employer for an annuity contract described in section 403(b).

SPECIAL RULES

The term "qualified employer plan"— shall include any plan which was (or was determined to be) a qualified employer plan or government plan, but shall not include a plan described in subsection (e)(7).

GOVERNMENT PLAN

The term "government plan" means any plan, whether or not qualified, established and maintained for its employees by the United States, by a State or political subdivision thereof, or by an agency or instrumentality of any of the foregoing.

SPECIAL RULES FOR LOANS, ETC., FROM CERTAIN CONTRACTS

For purposes of this subsection, any amount received as a loan under a contract purchased under a qualified employer plan (and any assignment or pledge with respect to such a contract) shall be treated as a loan under such employer plan.

10-PERCENT PENALTY FOR PREMATURE DISTRIBUTIONS FROM ANNUITY CONTRACTS IMPOSITION OF PENALTY

If any taxpayer receives any amount under an annuity contract, the taxpayer's tax under this chapter for the taxable year in which such amount is received shall be increased by an amount equal to 10 percent of the portion of such amount which is includible in gross income.

SUBSECTION NOT TO APPLY TO CERTAIN DISTRIBUTIONS

Paragraph (1) shall not apply to any distribution—

made on or after the date on which the taxpayer attains age 59½, made on or after the death of the holder (or, where the holder is not an individual), the death of the primary annuitant (as defined in subsection (s)(6)(B)), attributable to the taxpayer's becoming disabled within the meaning of subsection (m)(7),

which is a part of a series of substantially equal periodic payments (not less frequently than annually) made for the life (or life expectancy) of the taxpayer or the joint lives (or joint life expectancies) of such taxpayer and his designated beneficiary, from a plan, contract, account, trust, or annuity described in subsection (e)(5)(D), allocable to investment in the contract before August 14, 1982, or under a qualified funding asset (within the meaning of section 130(d), but without regard to whether there is a qualified assignment),

to which subsection (t) applies (without regard to paragraph (2) thereof), under an immediate annuity contract (within the meaning of section 72(u)(4)), or which is purchased by an employer upon the termination of a plan described in section 401(a) or 403(a) and which is held by the employer until such time as the employee separates from service.

CHANGE IN SUBSTANTIALLY EQUAL PAYMENTS

If—paragraph (1) does not apply to a distribution by reason of paragraph (2)(D), and the series of payments under such paragraph are subsequently modified (other than by reason of death or disability)—before the close of the 5-year period beginning on the date of the first payment and after the taxpayer attains age 59½, or before the taxpayer attains age 59½,

the taxpayer's tax for the 1st taxable year in which such modification occurs shall be increased by an amount, determined under regulations, equal to the tax which (but for paragraph (2)(D)) would have been imposed, plus interest for the deferral period (within the meaning of subsection (t)(4)(B)).

CERTAIN RAILROAD RETIREMENT BENEFITS TREATED AS RECEIVED UNDER EMPLOYER PLANS

IN GENERAL

Notwithstanding any other provision of law, any benefit provided under the Railroad Retirement Act of 1974 (other than a tier 1 railroad retirement benefit) shall be treated for purposes of this title as a benefit provided under an employer plan which meets the requirements of section 401(a).

TIER 2 TAXES TREATED AS CONTRIBUTIONS

IN GENERAL

For purposes of paragraph (1)—

the tier 2 portion of the tax imposed by section 3201 (relating to tax on employees) shall be treated as an employee contribution, the tier 2 portion of the tax imposed by section 3211 (relating to tax on employee representatives) shall be treated as an employee contribution, and

the tier 2 portion of the tax imposed by section 3221 (relating to tax on employers) shall be treated as an employer contribution.

TIER 2 PORTION

For purposes of subparagraph (A)—

AFTER 1984

With respect to compensation paid after 1984, the tier 2 portion shall be the taxes imposed by sections 3201(b), 3211(a)(2), and 3221(b).

AFTER SEPTEMBER 30, 1981, AND BEFORE 1985

With respect to compensation paid before 1985 for services rendered after September 30, 1981, the tier 2 portion shall be—so much of the tax imposed by section 3201 as is determined at the 2 percent rate, and so much of the taxes imposed by sections 3211 and 3221 as is determined at the 11.75 percent rate. With respect to compensation paid for services rendered after December 31, 1983, and before 1985, subclause (I) shall be applied by substituting "2.75 percent" for "2 percent" and subclause (II) shall be applied by substituting "12.75 percent" for "11.75 percent."

BEFORE OCTOBER 1, 1981

With respect to compensation paid for services rendered during any period before October 1, 1981, the tier 2 portion shall be the excess (if any) of—

the tax imposed for such period by section 3201, 3211, or 3221, as the case may be (other than any tax imposed with respect to man-hours), over the tax which would have been imposed by such section for such period had the rates of the comparable taxes imposed by chapter 21 for such period applied under such section.

CONTRIBUTIONS NOT ALLOCABLE TO SUPPLEMENTAL ANNUITY OR WINDFALL BENEFITS

For purposes of paragraph (1) no amount treated as an employee contribution under this paragraph shall be allocated to—

any supplemental annuity paid under section 2(b) of the Railroad Retirement Act of 1974, or any benefit paid under section 3(h), 4(e), or 4(h) of such Act.

TIER 1 RAILROAD RETIREMENT BENEFIT

For purposes of paragraph (1), the term "tier 1 railroad retirement benefit" has the meaning given such term by section 86(d)(4).

REQUIRED DISTRIBUTIONS WHERE HOLDER DIES BEFORE ENTIRE INTEREST IS DISTRIBUTED

IN GENERAL

A contract shall not be treated as an annuity contract for purposes of this title unless it provides that—if any holder of such contract dies on or after the annuity starting date and before the entire interest in such contract has been distributed, the remaining portion of such interest will be distributed at least as rapidly as under the method of distributions being used as of the date of his death, and if any holder of such contract dies before the annuity starting date, the entire interest in such contract will be distributed within 5 years after the death of such holder.

EXCEPTION FOR CERTAIN AMOUNTS PAYABLE OVER LIFE OF BENEFICIARY

If—any portion of the holder's interest is payable to (or for the benefit of) a designated beneficiary. Such portion will be distributed (in accordance with regulations) over the life of such designated beneficiary (or over a period not extending beyond the life expectancy of such beneficiary), and such distributions begin not later than 1 year after the date of the holder's death or such later date as the Secretary may by regulations prescribe, then for purposes of paragraph (1), the portion referred to in subparagraph (A) shall be treated as distributed on the day on which such distributions begin.

SPECIAL RULE WHERE SURVIVING SPOUSE IS BENEFICIARY

If the designated beneficiary referred to in paragraph (2)(A) is the surviving spouse of the holder of the contract, paragraphs (1) and (2) shall be applied by treating such spouse as the holder of such contract.

DESIGNATED BENEFICIARY

For purposes of this subsection, the term "designated beneficiary" means any individual designated a beneficiary by the holder of the contract.

EXCEPTION FOR CERTAIN ANNUITY CONTRACTS

This subsection shall not apply to any annuity contract—
    which is provided—under a plan described in section 401(a) which includes a trust exempt from tax under section 501, or under a plan described in section 403(a), which is described in section 403(b), which is an individual retirement annuity or provided under an individual retirement account or annuity, or which is a qualified funding asset (as defined in section 130(d), but without regard to whether there is a qualified assignment).

SPECIAL RULE WHERE HOLDER IS CORPORATION OR OTHER NONINDIVIDUAL

IN GENERAL

For purposes of this subsection, if the holder of the contract is not an individual, the primary annuitant shall be treated as the holder of the contract.

PRIMARY ANNUITANT

For purposes of subparagraph (A), the term "primary annuitant" means the individual, the events in the life of whom are of primary importance in affecting the timing or amount of the payout under the contract.

TREATMENT OF CHANGES IN PRIMARY ANNUITANT WHERE HOLDER OF CONTRACT IS NOT AN INDIVIDUAL

For purposes of this subsection, in the case of a holder of an annuity contract which is not an individual, if there is a change in a primary annuitant (as defined in paragraph (6)(B)), such change shall be treated as the death of the holder.

10-PERCENT ADDITIONAL TAX ON EARLY DISTRIBUTIONS FROM QUALIFIED RETIREMENT PLANS

IMPOSITION OF ADDITIONAL TAX

If any taxpayer receives any amount from a qualified retirement plan (as defined in section 4974C), the taxpayer's tax under this chapter for the taxable year in which such amount is received shall be increased by an amount equal to 10 percent of the portion of such amount which is includible in gross income.

SUBSECTION NOT TO APPLY TO CERTAIN DISTRIBUTIONS

Except as provided in paragraphs (3) and (4), paragraph (10 shall not apply to any of the following distributions:

IN GENERAL

Distributions which are—made on or after the date on which the employee attains age 59½, made to a beneficiary (or to the estate of the employee) on or after the death of the employee, attributable to the employee's being disabled within the meaning of subsection (m)(7), part of a series of substantially equal periodic payments (not less frequently than annually) made for the life (or life expectancy) of the employee or the joint lives (or joint life expectancies) of such employee and his designated beneficiary, made to an employee after separation from service after attainment of age 55, or dividends paid with respect to stock of a corporation which are described in section 404(k).

MEDICAL EXPENSES

Distributions made to the employee (other than distributions described in subparagraph (A) or (C)) to the extent such distributions do not exceed the amount allowable as a deduction under section 213 to the employee for amounts paid during the taxable year for medical care (determined without regard to whether the employee itemizes deductions for such taxable year).

PAYMENTS TO ALTERNATE PAYEES PURSUANT TO QUALIFIED DOMESTIC RELATIONS ORDERS

Any distribution to an alternate payee pursuant to a qualified domestic relations order (within the meaning of section 414(p)(1)).

LIMITATIONS

CERTAIN EXCEPTIONS NOT TO APPLY TO INDIVIDUAL RETIREMENT PLANS

Subparagraphs (A)(v), (B), and (C), of paragraph (2) shall not apply to distributions from an individual retirement plan.

PERIODIC PAYMENTS UNDER QUALIFIED PLANS MUST BEGIN AFTER SEPARATION

Paragraph (2)(A)(iv) shall not apply to any amount paid from a trust described in section 401(a) which is exempt from tax under section 501(a) or from a contract described in section 72(e)(5)(D)(ii) unless the series of payments begins after the employee separates from service.

CHANGE IN SUBSTANTIALLY EQUAL PAYMENTS
IN GENERAL

If—paragraph (1) does not apply to a distribution by reason of paragraph (2)(A)(iv), and the series of payments under such paragraph are subsequently modified (other than by reason of death or disability) before the close of the 5-year period beginning with the date of the first payment and after the employee attains age 59, or before the employee attains age 59½,

the taxpayer's tax for the 1st taxable year in which such modification occurs shall be increased by an amount, determined under regulations, equal to the tax which (but for paragraph (2)(A)(iv)) would have been imposed, plus interest for the deferral period.

DEFERRAL PERIOD

For purposes of this paragraph, the term "deferral period" means the period beginning with the taxable year in which (without regard to paragraph (2)(A)(iv)) the distribution would have been includible in gross income and ending with the taxable year in which the modification described in subparagraph (A) occurs.

EMPLOYEE

For purposes of this subsection, the term "employee" includes any participant, and in the case of an individual retirement plan, the individual for whose benefit such plan was established.

TREATMENT OF ANNUITY CONTRACTS NOT
HELD BY NATURAL PERSONS IN GENERAL

If any annuity contract is held by a person who is not a natural person—such contract shall not be treated as an annuity contract for purposes of this subtitle (other than subchapter L), and the income on the contract for any taxable year of the policyholder shall be treated as ordinary income received or accrued by the owner during such taxable year. For purposes of this paragraph, holding by a trust or other entity as an agent for a natural person shall not be taken into account.

INCOME ON THE CONTRACT IN GENERAL

For purposes of paragraph (1), the term "income on the contract" means, with respect to any taxable year of the policyholder, the excess of—
the sum of the net surrender value of the contract as of the close of the taxable year plus all distributions under the contract received during the taxable year or any prior taxable year, reduced by the sum of the amount of net premiums under the contract for the taxable year and prior taxable years and amounts includible in gross income for prior taxable years with respect to such contract under this subsection. Where necessary to prevent the avoidance of this subsection, the Secretary may substitute "fair market value of the contract" for "net surrender value of the contract" each place it appears in the preceding sentence.

NET PREMIUMS

For purposes of this paragraph, the term "net premiums" means the amount of premiums paid under the contract reduced by any policyholder dividends.

EXCEPTIONS

This subsection shall not apply to any annuity contract which—
is acquired by the estate of a decedent by reason of the death of the decedent, is held under a plan described in section 401(a) or 403(a), under a program described in section 403(b), or under an individual retirement plan, is a qualified funding asset (as defined in section 130(d), but without regard to whether there is a qualified assignment), is purchased by an employer upon the termination of a plan described in section 401(a) or 403(a) and which is held by the employer until all amounts under such contract are distributed to the employee for whom such contract was purchased or the employee's beneficiary, or is an immediate annuity.

IMMEDIATE ANNUITY

For purposes of this subsection, the term "immediate annuity" means an annuity—which is purchased with a single premium or annuity consideration, the annuity starting date (as defined in subsection (c)(4)) of which commences no later than 1 year from the date of the purchase of the annuity, and which provides for a series of substantially equal periodic payments (to be made not less frequently than annually) during the annuity period.

10-PERCENT ADDITIONAL TAX FOR TAXABLE DISTRIBUTIONS FROM MODIFIED ENDOWMENT CONTRACTS

IMPOSITION OF ADDITIONAL TAX

If any taxpayer receives any amount under a modified endowment contract (as defined in section 7702A), the taxpayer's tax under this chapter for the taxable year in which such amount is received shall be increased by an amount equal to 10 percent of the portion of such amount which is includible in gross income.

SUBSECTION NOT TO APPLY TO CERTAIN DISTRIBUTIONS

Paragraph (1) shall not apply to any distribution—
made on or after the date on which the taxpayer attains age 59½, which is attributable to the taxpayer's becoming disabled (within the meaning of subsection (m)(7)), or which is part of a series of substantially equal periodic payments (not less frequently than annually) made for the life (or life expectancy) of the taxpayer or the joint lives (or joint life expectancies) of such taxpayer and his beneficiary.

CROSS REFERENCE

For limitation on adjustments to basis of annuity contracts sold, see section 1021.

INTERNAL REVENUE CODE SECTION 1035

CERTAIN EXCHANGES OF INSURANCE POLICIES

GENERAL RULES

No gain or loss shall be recognized on the exchange of—a contract of life insurance for another contract of life insurance or for an endowment or annuity contract; or a contract of endowment insurance (A) for another contract of endowment insurance which provides for regular payments beginning at a date not later than the date payments would have begun under the contract exchanged, or (B) for an annuity contract; or an annuity contract for an annuity contract.

DEFINITIONS

For the purpose of this section—

ENDOWMENT CONTRACT

A contract of endowment insurance is a contract with an insurance company which depends in part on the life expectancy of the insured, but which may be payable in full in a single payment during his life.

ANNUITY CONTRACT

An annuity contract is a contract to which paragraph (1) applies but which may be payable during the life of the annuitant only in installments.

LIFE INSURANCE CONTRACT

A contract of life insurance is a contract to which paragraph (1) applies but which is not ordinarily payable in full during the life of the insured.

CROSS REFERENCES

For rules relating to recognition of gain or loss where an exchange is not solely in kind, see subsections (b) and (c) of section 1031. For rules relating to the basis of property acquired in an exchange described in subsection (a), see subsection (d) of section 1031.

INTERNAL REVENUE CODE SECTION 2033
PROPERTY IN WHICH THE DECEDENT HAD AN INTEREST

The value of the gross estate shall include the value of all property to the extent of the interest therein of the decedent at the time of his death.

INTERNAL REVENUE CODE SECTION 2039
ANNUITIES, GENERAL

The gross estate shall include the value of an annuity or other payment receivable by any beneficiary by reason of surviving the decedent under any form of contract or agreement entered into after March 3, 1931 (other than as insurance under policies on the life of the decedent), if, under such contract or agreement, an annuity or other payment was payable to the decedent, or the decedent possessed the right to receive such annuity or payment, either alone or in conjunction with another for his life or for any period not ascertainable without reference to his death or for any period which does not in fact end before his death.

AMOUNT INCLUDIBLE

Subsection (a) shall apply to only such part of the value of the annuity or other payment receivable under such contract or agreement as is proportionate to that part of the purchase price therefor contributed by the decedent. For purposes of this section, any contribution by the decedent's employer or former employer to the purchase price of such contract or agreement (whether or not to an employee's trust or fund forming part of a pension, annuity, retirement, bonus or profit sharing plan) shall be considered to be contributed by the decedent if made by reason of his employment.

accumulated value The value of all amounts accumulated under the contract prior to the annuity date.

accumulation unit A measure of your ownership interest in the contract prior to the annuity date.

accumulation unit value The value of each accumulation unit which is calculated each valuation period.

adjusted death benefit The sum of all net purchase payments made during the first six contract years, less any partial withdrawals taken. For an enhanced death benefit with a six-year step up each subsequent six-year period, the adjusted death benefit will be the death benefit on the last day of the previous six-year period plus any net purchase payments made, less any partial withdrawals taken during the current six-year period. After the Annuitant reaches age 75, the adjusted death benefit will remain equal to the death benefit on the last day of the six-year period before age 75 occurs plus any net purchase payments subsequently made, less any partial withdrawals subsequently taken.

administrative fee An annual fee, usually 0.15 percent or less of the daily sub-account asset value, charged to reimburse administrative expenses.

annual contract fee The annual fee charged by the company to cover the cost of administering each contract. It will be deducted on each contract anniversary and upon surrender, on a pro rata basis, from each sub-account.

annual insurance company expenses Charges included in annuity contracts for insurance companies' annual expenses. In addition to the asset management fees, there are three other annual charges: administrative fee, annual policy fee, and mortality and expense risk.

annual interest income The annual dollar income for a bond or savings account is calculated by multiplying the bond's coupon rate by its face value.

annual policy fee (maintenance fee) An annual fee, usually $50 or less, charged for the maintenance of the annuity records. The fee pays accounting, customer reporting, and other general expenses associated with financial record-keeping requirements.

annualized return The total return on an investment or portfolio over a period of time other than one year, restated as an equivalent return for a one-year period. Also called compound return.

annuitant The person whose life is used to determine the duration of any annuity payments and upon whose death, prior to the annuity date, benefits under the contract are paid.

annuitant's beneficiary The person(s) to whom any benefits are due upon the annuitant's death prior to the annuity date.

annuitization   An income paid-out option is refered to as annuitization.

annuity   A contract between an insurer and recipient (annuitant) whereby the insurer guarantees to pay the recipient a stream of income in exchange for premium payment(s).

annuity date   The date on which annuity payments begin. It is always the first day of the month the contract owner specifies.

annuity payment   One of a series of payments made under an annuity payment option.

annuity payment option   One of several ways in which withdrawals from the contract may be made. Under a fixed annuity option the dollar amount of each annuity payment does not change over time. Under a variable annuity option the dollar amount of each annuity payment may change over time, depending upon the investment experience of the portfolio or portfolios you choose. Annuity payments are based on the contract's accumulated value as of 10 business days prior to the annuity date.

annuity unit   Unit of measure used to calculate variable annuity payments.

annuity unit value   The value of each annuity unit, which is calculated each valuation period.

asset allocation   The decision as to how a customer should be invested among major asset classes in order to increase expected risk-adjusted return. Asset allocation may be two-way (stocks and bonds), three-way (stocks, bonds, and cash), or many-way (e.g., value mutual funds, growth mutual funds, small mutual funds, cash, foreign mutual funds, foreign bonds, real estate, and venture capital).

asset class   Assets composed of financial instruments with similar characteristics.

asset-class investing   The disciplined purchase of groups of securities with similar risk/reward profiles. This strategy is based on valid academic research and its results are predictable rather than random.

average daily trading   The average daily trading is the number of shares of stock traded in the preceding calendar month, multiplied by the current price and divided by 20 trading days.

average return   The measure of the price of an asset, along with its income or yield, on average over a specific time period. The arithmetic mean is the simple average of the returns in a series. The arithmetic mean is the appropriate measure of typical performance for a single period.

back-end load   A fee charged at redemption by a mutual fund or a variable annuity to a buyer of shares.

bailout rate   A feature offered on some annuities that allows the customer to surrender the annuity with no penalty if the interest rate falls below a certain floor.

balanced index   A market index that serves as a basis of comparison for balanced portfolios. The balanced index used by most institutions is comprised of a 60 percent weighting of the S&P 500 Index and a 40 percent weighting of the SLH Government/Corporate Bond Index. The balanced index relates unmanaged market returns to a balanced portfolio more precisely than either a stock or a bond index would alone.

balanced mutual fund A mutual fund that includes two or more asset classes other than cash. In a typical balanced mutual fund, the asset classes are equities and fixed-income securities. Many "boutique" investment managers are balanced managers, which permits them to tailor the securities in a portfolio to the specific clients' cashflow needs and objectives. Balanced portfolios are often used by major mutual funds. They provide great flexibility.

basis point One basis point is 1/100 of a percentage point, or 0.01 percent. Basis points are often used to express changes or differences in yields, returns, or interest rates. Thus, if a portfolio has a total return of 10 percent versus 7 percent for the S&P 500, the portfolio is said to have outperformed the S&P 500 by 300 basis points.

bear market A prolonged period of falling stock prices. There is no consensus on what constitutes a bear market or bear leg. SEI, one of the most widely used performance measurement services, normally defines a bear market or bear leg as a drop of at least 15 percent over two back-to-back quarters.

beginning value The market value of a portfolio at the inception of the period being measured by the customer statement.

beneficiary Similar to the beneficiary of a life insurance policy, the annuity contract beneficiary receives a death benefit when another party to the annuity contract dies prior to the date upon which the annuity begins paying out benefits.

benchmark A standard by which investment performance or trading execution can be judged. The most widely used performance benchmark is the total return of the S&P 500.

beta Beta is the linear relationship between the return on the security and the return on the market. By definition, the market, usually measured by the S&P 500 Index, has beta of 1.00. Any stock or portfolio with a higher beta is generally more volatile than the market, while any with a lower beta is generally less volatile than the market.

bond rating Method of evaluating the possibility of default by a bond issuer. Standard & Poor's, Moody's Investors Service, and Fitch Investors Service analyze the financial strength of each bond's issuer, whether a corporation or a government body. Their ratings range from AAA (highly unlikely to default) to D (in default). Bonds rated B or below are not investment grade—in other words, institutions that invest other people's money may not under most state laws buy them.

bull market A prolonged period of rising stock prices. SEI, one of the most widely used performance measurement services, normally defines a bull market or bull leg as a rise of at least 15 percent over two back-to-back quarters.

business day A day when the New York Stock Exchange is open for trading.

capital appreciation or depreciation An increase or decrease in the value of a mutual fund or stock due to a change in the market price of the fund. For example, a stock that rises from $50 to $55 has capital appreciation of 10 percent. Dividends are not included in appreciation. If the price of the stock fell to $45, it would have depreciation of 10 percent.

charitable remainder trust (CRT) A trust instrument that provides for specific payment to one or more individuals, with an irrevocable remainder in the trust property to be paid to or held for a charity.

commissions Fees charged for buying or selling securities.

company Refers to the insurance company issuing the annuity.

compounding The reinvestment of dividends and/or interest and capital gains. This means that over time, dividends and interest and capital gains grow exponentially. For example, $100 earning compound interest at 10 percent a year would accumulate to $110 at the end of the first year and $121 at the end of the second year based on this formula: compound sum = [principal (1 + interest rate)] number of periods.

conservative A characteristic relating to a mutual fund, stock, or investment style. There is no precise definition of the term, but generally it is used when the mutual fund manager's emphasis is on the below-market betas.

Consumer Price Index (CPI) An index maintained by the Bureau of Labor Statistics that measures the changes in the cost of a specified group of consumer products relative to a base period. Because it represents the rate of inflation, the CPI can be used as a general benchmark for gauging the maintenance of purchasing power.

contract The legal agrement between the insurance company and the owner of the annuity.

contract anniversary Any anniversary of the contract date.

contract date The date of issue of this contract.

contract owner ("you," "your") The person or persons designated in the contract as the contract owner. The term shall also include any person named as joint owner. A joint owner shares ownership in all respects with the contract owner. Prior to the annuity date, the contract owner has the right to assign ownership, designate beneficiaries, make permitted withdrawals and exchanges among sub-accounts and guaranteed rate options.

contract year A period of 12 months starting with the contract date or any contract anniversary.

contrarian An investment approach characterized by buying securities that are out of favor.

correction A reversal in the price of a stock, or the stock market as a whole, within a larger trend. Although most often thought of as a decline within an overall market rise, a correction can also be a temporary rise in the midst of a longer-term decline.

coupon The periodic interest payment on a bond. When expressed as an annual percentage, it is called the coupon rate. When multiplied by the face value of the bond, the coupon rate gives the annual interest income. See also **annual interest income**.

current return on equity (ROE) A ratio that measures profitability as the return on common stockholders' equity. It is calculated by dividing the reported earnings per share for the latest 12-month period by the book value per share.

current yield This is a bond's annual interest payment as a percentage of its current market price. The current yield is calculated by dividing the annual coupon interest for a bond by the current market price. The coupon rate and the current yield on a bond are equal when the bond is selling at par. Thus, a $1000 bond with a coupon of 10 percent that is currently selling at $1000 will have a current yield of 10.0 percent. However, if the bond's price drops to $800 the current yield becomes 12.5 percent.

death benefit The greater of the contract's accumulated value (on the date the company receives due proof of death of the annuitant) or the adjusted death benefit. If any portion of the contract's accumulated value is derived from the multi-year guaranteed rate option, that portion of the accumulated value will be adjusted by a positive or negative market value adjustment factor.

deferred annuity An annuity whose contract provides that payments to the annuitant be postponed until a number of periods have elapsed, for example, when the annuitant attains a certain age.

diversification A strategy for investing in different companies or different asset classes to reduce the risks inherent in investing in a single company or class. In broad terms, a customer might diversify his or her investments among mutual funds, real estate, international investments, and money market instruments. A mutual fund might diversify by investing in many companies in many different industry groups. Diversification also can refer to the way large sponsors reduce risk by using multiple mutual fund styles.

dividend The payment from a company's earnings normally paid on common shares declared by a company's board of directors to be distributed pro rata among the shares outstanding.

dollar cost averaging A system of buying stocks or mutual funds at regular intervals with a fixed dollar amount. Under this system an investor buys by the dollar's worth rather than by the number of shares.

Dow Jones Industrial Average (DJIA) A price-weighted average of 30 leading blue-chip industrial stocks, calculated by adding the prices of the 30 stocks and adjusting by a divisor, which reflects any stock dividends or splits. The DJIA is the most widely quoted index of the stock market, but it is not widely used as a benchmark for evaluating performance. The S&P 500 Index, which is more representative of the market, is the benchmark most widely used by performance measurement services.

earnings per share (EPS) growth The annualized rate of growth in reported earnings per share of stock.

economies of scale A typical U-shaped, long-term average cost curve. As a company's outpot is increased, the costs generally go down.

emerging growth fund This implies new companies that may be relatively small in size with the potential to grow much larger.

emerging growth mutual funds A mutual fund consisting of industries and companies whose growth rates are likely to be both rapid and independent of the overall stock market. Emerging, of course, means new. This implies such companies may be relatively small in size with the potential to grow much larger. Such stocks are generally much more volatile than the stock market in general and require constant, close attention to developments.

equities Common or preferred stocks. Claims of both common and preferred stockholders are junior to claims of bondholders or other creditors of the company.

Holders of common stock assume the greater risk but generally exercise a greater degree of control and may gain the greater reward in the form of dividend growth and capital appreciation.

exchange One exchange will be deemed to occur with each voluntary transfer from any sub-account or general account guaranteed option.

exchange privilege A shareholder's right to switch from one mutual fund to another within one fund family, often done at no additional charge. This enables investors to put their money in an aggressive growth stock fund, for example, when they expect the market to turn up strongly, then switch to a money market fund when they anticipate a downturn.

execution price The negotiated price at which a security is purchased or sold.

fixed annuities The word "fixed" is used to describe the type of annuity referred to by the interest rate paid by the issuing insurance company on the fund's place in the annuity. The fixed annuity offers security in that the rate of return is certain. Typically, with a fixed annuity the insurance company declares a current interest rate and sets the interest rate.

fixed income mutual fund A mutual fund that invests in bonds, notes, and other debt instruments. Managers of the funds have a broad range of styles, involving market timing, swapping to gain quality or yield, setting up maturity ladders, etc. A typical division of the fixed-income market is between short (up to 3 years), intermediate (3 to 15 years), and long (15 to 30 years).

401(k) section of the Internal Revenue Code In its most simple terms, a 401(k) plan is a before-tax employee saving plan.

front-end load A fee charged when an investor buys a mutual fund or a variable annuity.

fundamentals The financial statistics that traditional analysts and many valuation models use. Fundamental data include stock, earnings, dividends, assets and liabilities, inventories, debt, etc. Fundamental data are in contrast to items used in technical analysis—such as price momentum, volume trends, and short sales statistics.

general account The account that contains all of a company's assets other than those held in separate accounts.

general account guaranteed option Any of the following three general account options offered by the contract and to which the contract owner may allocate net purchase payments: the one-year guaranteed rate option, the multi-year guaranteed rate option, and the guaranteed equity option. These options are available in most, but not all, states.

guaranteed rate options The one-year guaranteed rate option and the multi-year guaranteed rate option.

income growth mutual fund The primary purpose in security selection here is to achieve a current yield significantly higher than the S&P 500. The stability of the dividend and the rate of growth of the dividends are also of concern to the income buyer. These portfolios may own more utilities and fewer high-tech companies and may own convertible preferreds and convertible bonds.

index fund A passively managed mutual fund portfolio designed and computer-controlled to track the performance of a certain index, such as the S&P 500. In general, such mutual funds have performance within a few basis points of the target index. The most popular index mutual funds are those that track the S&P 500, but special index funds, such as those based on the Russell 1000 or the Wilshire 5000, are also available.

interest-rate guarantee A guarantee that the renewal rate will never fall below a particular level. Typical policies today have a 4 percent to 5 percent guarantee.

intrinsic value The theoretical valuation or price for a stock. The valuation is determined using a valuation theory or model. The resulting value is compared with the current market price. If the intrinsic value is greater than the market price, the stock is considered undervalued.

investment style A disciplined process of managing money in financial instruments so as to gain a return.

joint owner The person or persons designated as the contract owner in the contract. The term also includes any person named as joint owner. A joint owner shares ownership in all respects with the contract owner.

load funds A mutual fund that is sold for a sales charge (load) by a brokerage firm or other sales representative. Such funds may be stock, bond, or commodity funds, with conservative or aggressive objectives. The stated advantage of a load fund is that the salesperson will explain the fund to the customer and advise him or her when it is appropriate to sell as well as when to buy more shares.

lump-sum distribution Single payment to a beneficiary covering the entire amount of an agreement. Participants in individual retirement accounts, pension plans, profit-sharing, and executive stock option plans generally can opt for a lump-sum distribution if the taxes are not too burdensome when they become eligible.

management fee Charge against investor assets for managing the portfolio of an open- or closed-end mutual fund as well as for such services as shareholder relations or administration. The fee, as disclosed in the prospectus, is a fixed percentage of the fund's asset value, typically 1 percent or less per year.

market bottom The date that the bear leg of a market cycle reaches its low, not identified until some time after the fact. Market bottoms can also be defined as the month- or quarter-end closest to the actual bottom date.

market capitalization The current value of a company determined by multiplying the latest available number of outstanding common shares by the current market price of a share. For example, on December 29, 1989, IBM had about 590 million shares outstanding and the stock closed at $94.13. Thus, its market capitalization was $55 billion. Market cap is also an indication of the trading liquidity of a particular issue.

market timing The attempt to base investment decisions on the expected direction of the market. If stocks are expected to decline, the timer may elect to hold a portion of the portfolio in cash equivalents or bonds. Timers may base their decisions on fundamentals (e.g., selling stocks when the market's price-to-book ratio reaches a certain level), on technical considerations (such as declining momentum or excessive investor optimism), or on a combination of both.

market value The market or liquidation value of a given security or of an entire pool of assets.

market value adjustment factor The formula applied to the accumulated value in order to determine the net amount of any transfer or surrender under the multi-year guaranteed rate.

money market fund A mutual fund invested in short-term fixed instruments and cash equivalents. These instruments make up the portfolio and the objective is to maximize principal protection. Even though these accounts have short-term (one-day) liquidity, they typically pay more like 90- to 180-day CDs versus passbook or one-week CDs.

mortality and expense risk (M&E) An annual charge, 1.00 to 1.50 percent of the daily asset value of each sub-account, charged for the mortality risk that arises from the obligation to pay guaranteed death benefits or guaranteed lifetime income payments to annuitants.

mutual fund A mutual fund is an investment company that makes investments on behalf of its participants who share common financial goals. The fund pools your money with others who have different amounts to invest.

mutual fund families A number of funds with different investment objectives offered by the same sponsor or company. For example, a mutual fund family may include a money market fund, a government bond fund, a corporate bond fund, a blue-chip stock fund, and a more speculative stock fund. If an investor buys a fund in the family, he or she is allowed to exchange that fund for another in the same family, usually with no additional sales charge.

National Association of Securities Dealers, Inc. (NASD) The principal association of over-the-counter (OTC) brokers and dealers that establishes legal and ethical standards of conduct for its members. NASD was established in 1939 to regulate the OTC market in much the same manner as organized exchanges monitor actions of their members.

net asset value (NAV) The market value of each share of a mutual fund. This figure is derived by taking a fund's total assets (securities, cash, and receivables), deducting liabilities, and then dividing that total by the number of shares outstanding.

Net Income Makeup Charitable Remainder Unitrusts (NIMCRUT) An income-only trust that provides for any income deficiencies in past years to be made up to the extent trust income exceeds the amount of the specific percentage in later years.

net purchase payment Any purchase payment less the applicable premium tax, if any.

net trade Generally, an over-the-counter trade involving no explicit commission. The investment advisor's compensation is in the spread between the cost of the security and the price paid by the customer. Also, a trade in which shares are exchanged directly with the issuer.

no-load funds Mutual fund offered by an open-end investment company that imposes no sales charge (load) on its shareholders. Investors buy shares in no-load funds directly from the fund companies, rather than through a broker, as is done in load funds. Because no broker is used, no advice is given on when to buy or sell.

nominal return The actual current dollar growth in an asset's value over a given period. See also **total return** and **real return**.

non-qualified contract An annuity which is not used as part of or in connection with a qualified retirement plan.

over-the-counter A market made between securities dealers who act either as principal or broker for their clients. This is the principal market for U.S. government and municipal bonds.

owner's designated beneficiary The person to whom ownership of this contract passes upon the contract owner's death, unless the contract owner was also the annuitant—in which case the annuitant's beneficiary is entitled to the death benefit. (Note: This transfer of ownership to the owner's designated beneficiary will generally not be subject to probate but will be subject to estate and inheritance taxes. Consult with your tax and estate advisor to learn which rules will apply to you.)

packaged products Specific types of products underwritten and packaged by manufacturing companies that can be bought and sold directly through those companies. Packaged products are not required to go through a clearing process. Packaged products include mutual funds, unit investment trusts (UITs), limited partnership interests, and annuities.

payee The contract owner, annuitant, annuitant's beneficiary, or any other person, estate, or legal entity to whom benefits are to be paid.

percentage points Used to describe the difference between two readings that are percentages. For example, if a portfolio's performance was 18.2 percent versus the S&P 500's 14.6, it outperformed the S&P by 3.6 percentage points.

portfolio A separate investment series of the funds. The term *portfolio* also refers to the sub-account that invests in the corresponding portfolio.

premium tax A regulatory tax that may be assessed by certain states on the purchase payments you make on a contract. The amount which the seller must pay as premium tax will be deducted from each purchase payment or from the contract's accumulated value as it is incurred.

price/earnings ratio (P/E) The current price divided by reported earnings per share of stock for the latest 12-month period. For example, a stock with earnings per share during the trailing year of $5 and currently selling at $50 per share has a price/earnings ratio of 10.

principal The original dollar amount invested.

proof of death (a) A certified death certificate; (b) a certified decree of a court of competent jurisdiction as to the finding of death; (c) a written statement by a medical doctor who attended the deceased; or (d) any other proof of death satisfactory to the company.

prospectus the document required by the Securities and Exchange Commission that accompanies the sale of a mutual fund or annuity, outlining risks associated with certain types of funds or securities, fees, and management. At the core of the prospectus is a description of the fund's investment objectives and the portfolio manager's philosophy.

purchase payment Any premium payment. The minimum initial purchase payment is $5000 for nonqualified contracts and $2000 for qualified contracts (or $50 monthly by payroll deduction for qualified contracts); each additional purchase payment must be at least $500 for nonqualified contracts or $50 for qualified contracts. Purchase payments may be made at any time prior to the annuity date as long as the annuitant is living.

qualified contract If an annuity contract is part of an employee benefit plan and has met certain requirements, it is "qualified" under the Internal Revenue Code. The contribution made into a qualified contract is tax deductible to the employer making the contribution and certain nondiscrimination requirements are met.

quality growth mutual fund A mutual fund that involves long-term investment in high quality growth stocks, some of which might be larger, emerging companies whereas others might be well-established household names. Such a portfolio might have volatility equal to or above that of the overall market, but less than that of an emerging growth portfolio.

quartile A ranking of comparative portfolio performance. The top 25 percent of mutual fund managers are in the 1st quartile, those ranking in the 26 percent to 50 percent range are in the 2nd quartile, from 51 percent to 75 percent in the 3rd quartile, and the lowest 25 percent in the 4th quartile.

real return The inflation-adjusted return on an asset. Inflation-adjusted returns are calculated by subtracting the rate of inflation from an asset's apparent, or nominal, return. For example, if common stocks earn a total return of 10.3 percent over a period of time, but inflation during that period is 3.1 percent, the real return is the difference: 7.2 percent.

reinvested dividends Dividends paid by a particular mutual fund that are reinvested in that same mutual fund. Some mutual funds offer automatic dividend reinvestment programs. In the complex equation theoretically used to determine the performance of the S&P 500, each company's dividend is reinvested in the stock of that company.

relative return The return of a stock or a mutual fund portfolio compared with some index, usually the S&P 500. For example, in 1989, American Brands had a total return of 12.2 percent in *absolute* terms. In isolation, that sounds good. After all, the historical annualized return on common stocks has been 10.3 percent. But because the S&P 500 had a return of 31.7 percent in 1989, American Brands underperformed the index in *relative* terms by 19.5 percentage points. Thus, its relative return was –19.5 percentage points.

renewal rate history A written indication, which the bank should supply, of how their renewal rates have held after the initial rate guarantee period. Also, the interest rate history an annuity company has offered to its owners.

right to cancel period The period during which the contract can be canceled and treated as void from the contract date.

risk   The potential to lose money or not to make money on an investment. A mutual fund portfolio has two types of risk. The first, called market risk, captures the amount of portfolio variability caused by events that have an impact on the market as a whole. The second is called investment risk. Investment risk is the actual variability or expected uncertainty of investment returns over a given period of time. This variability or uncertainty causes "rational" investors to expect higher returns on investments where the actual timing or amount of payoffs is not guaranteed.

risk-free rate of return   The return on an asset that is considered virtually without risk. U.S. government Treasury bills are typically used as the risk-free asset because of their short time horizon and the low probability of default.

Rule of 72   Shorthand for the principle that a 7.2 percent interest rate will double every 10 years.

Securities and Exchange Commission (SEC)   The keystone agency in the regulation of securities markets. It governs exchanges, over-the-counter markets, broker-dealers, the conduct of secondary markets, extension of credit in securities transactions, the conduct of corporate insiders, and principally the prohibition of fraud and manipulation in securities transactions.

securities investor protection corporation (SIPC)   A government-sponsored organization created in 1970 to insure investor accounts at brokerage firms in the event of the brokerage firm's insolvency and liquidation. The maximum insurance of $500,000, including a maximum of $100,000 in cash assets per account, covers customer losses due to brokerage house insolvency, not customer losses caused by security price fluctuations. SIPC coverage is conceptually similar to Federal Deposit Insurance Corporation coverage of customer accounts at commercial banks.

separate account   An account independent of the general account (general assets) of the company. The separate account invests in the portfolios.

Standard & Poor's (S&P) common stock rankings   The S&P rankings measure historical growth and stability of earnings and dividends. The system includes nine rankings: A+, A, and A- (above average); B+ (Average); B, B-, and C (below average); and NR (insufficient historical data or not amenable to the ranking process). As a matter of policy, S&P does not rank the stocks of foreign companies, investment companies, and certain finance-oriented companies.

Standard & Poor's (S&P) 500   The performance benchmark most widely used by sponsors, managers, and performance measurement services. This index includes 400 industrial stocks, 20 transportation stocks, 40 financial stocks, and 40 public utilities. Performance is measured on a capitalization-weighted basis.

standard deviation   Volatility can be statistically measured using standard deviation. Standard deviation describes how far from the mean, historic performance has been, either higher or lower. Mean is simply the middle point between the two historic extremes of the performance of the investment you are examining. The standard deviation measurement helps explain what the distribution of returns will likely be. The greater the range of returns, the greater the risk. Generally, the current price of a security reflects the expected total return of its investment and its perceived risk. The lower the risk, the lower the return expected.

strategic asset allocation Determines an appropriate asset mix for a customer based on long-term capital market conditions, expected returns, and risks.

sub-account That portion of the separate account that invests in shares of the fund's portfolios. Each sub-account will only invest in a single portfolio.

surrender charges Also known as back-end fees.

surrender value The accumulated value, adjusted to reflect any applicable market value adjustment for amounts allocated to the multi-year guaranteed rate option, less any early withdrawal charges for amounts allocated to the one-year guaranteed rate option, less any amount allocated to the guaranteed equity option, less any premium taxes incurred but not yet deducted.

systematic withdrawal plan A program in which shareholders receive payments from their mutual fund investments at regular intervals. Typically, these payments are drawn first from the fund's dividends and capital gains distribution, if any, and then from principal as needed.

12b-1 mutual fund Mutual fund that assesses shareholders for some of its promotion expenses. These funds are usually no-load, so no brokers are involved in the sale to the public. Instead, the funds normally rely on advertising and public relations to build their assets. The charge usually amounts to about 1 percent or less of a fund's assets. A 12b-1 fund must be specifically registered as such with the Securities and Exchange Commission, and the fact that such charges are levied must be disclosed.

technical analysis Any investment approach that judges the attractiveness of particular stocks or the market as a whole based on market data, such as price patterns, volume, momentum, or investor sentiment, as opposed to fundamental financial data, such as earnings dividends.

time-weighted rate of return The rate at which a dollar invested at the beginning of a period would grow if no additional capital were invested and no cash withdrawals were made. It provides an indication of value added by the investment manager and allows comparisons to the performance of other investment managers and market indices.

total return A standard measure of performance or return including both capital appreciation (or depreciation) and dividends or other income received. For example, Stock A is priced at $60 at the start of a year and pays an annual dividend of $4. If the stock moves up to $70 in price, the appreciation component is 16.7 percent, the yield component is 6.7 percent, and the total return is 23.4 percent. That oversimplification does not take into account any earnings on the reinvested dividends.

transaction costs Another term for execution costs. Total transaction costs (or the cost of buying and selling stocks) have three components: (1) the actual dollars paid to the broker in commissions, (2) the market impact—that is, the impact a manager's trade has on the market price for the stock (this varies with the size of the trade and the skill of the trader), and (3) the opportunity cost of the return (positive or negative) given up by not executing the trade instantaneously.

Treasury bills (T-bills) Promissory notes issued by the U.S. Treasury and sold through competitive bidding, with a short-term maturity date, usually 13 to 26 weeks. The return on T-bills has almost no variation, so it serves as a proxy for a "riskless" investment.

turnover The volume or percentage of buying or selling activity within a mutual fund portfolio relative to the mutual fund portfolio's size.

valuation period The period of time between the close of business on one business day and the close of business on the following business day. The accumulation unit value, which measures the relative value of a contract, is calculated each valuation period.

value added Returns over and above those of the stock market.

value mutual fund A mutual fund in which the manager has used various tests to determine an intrinsic value for a given security and has tried to purchase the security substantially below that value. The goal and hope are that the stock price in the fund will ultimately rise to the stock's fair value or above. Price-to-earnings, price-to-sales, price-to-cashflow, price-to-book value, and price-to-breakup value (or true net asset value) are some of the ratios examined in such an approach.

variable annuities Insurance-based investment products, which like other forms of annuities allow for growth of invested premiums to be free from taxation until withdrawals are made from the contract. Unique to variable annuities are several forms of investment alternatives that vary in their potential for reward and risk. Variable annuity choices are broad enough that an investor can employ either an aggressive or conservative approach, or a combination of both, while enjoying the benefits of tax-deferred growth. Guarantee of principal from loss upon death of the owner is covered by a death benefit provision.

variable annuity accumulation and distribution phases Two phases of the "life" of an annuity. The accumulation phase is the period in which contributions are made, either as a lump sum or in systematic payments. The contributions are invested in either a fixed or variable annuity. The assets compound tax-deferred until the contract owner makes the decision to distribute the assets (distribution phase), either in a lump sum or systematically.

volatility The extent to which market values and investment returns are uncertain or fluctuate. Another word for risk, volatility is gauged using such measures as beta, mean absolute deviation, and standard deviation.

withdrawal provisions Provides for the ability to withdraw funds from the annuity. Typically, the withdrawal provision defines penalty-free withdrawal options: Does the policy have a 10 percent free withdrawal provision? Is that provision cumulative? In other words, if the customer doesn't use the 10 percent for the first year, can he or she get 10 percent free the next year?

yield (current yield) For stocks, yield is the percentage return paid in dividends on a common or preferred stock, calculated by dividing the indicated annual dividend by the market price of the stock. For example, if a stock sells for $40 and pays a dividend of $2 per share, it has a yield of 5 percent ($2 divided by $40). For bonds, the coupon rate of interest divided by the market price is called current yield. For example, a bond selling for $1000 with a 10 percent coupon offers a 10 percent current yield. If the same bond were selling for $500, it would offer a 20 percent yield to an investor who bought it for $500. (As a bond's price falls, its yield rises, and vice versa.)

yield to maturity The discount rate that equates the present value of the bond's cashflows (semiannual coupon payments and the redemption value) with the market price. The yield to maturity will actually be earned if (1) the investor holds the bond to maturity and (2) the investor is able to reinvest all coupon payments at a rate equal to the yield to maturity. When a bond is selling at par, the yield to maturity and the coupon rate are equal.

INDEX